CLEARING

CLEARING

Your guide to maintaining healthy energy

Kerrie Erwin

ROCKPOOL
PUBLISHING

A Rockpool book

PO Box 252

Summer Hill

NSW 2130

Australia

www.rockpoolpublishing.com.au

www.facebook.com/RockpoolPublishing

Follow us! **f** 🄾 rockpoolpublishing

Tag your images with #rockpoolpublishing

ISBN 978-1-925429-98-5

First published in 2019

Design by Jessica Le, Rockpool Publishing

Edited by Kathryn Lamberton

Printed and bound in China

10 9 8 7 6 5 4 3 2 1

Dedication

Love and Blessing to the brave souls who follow the light, keep the faith and understand the gift of love, healing, prayer and miracles.

And to my loving protective spirit team and writing guide Leon, forever faithful in my sacred circle of spiritual friendships.

AMEN

White light is powerful, more than any type of dark energy. It is the power of Universal Love in its higher form.

Call on the light, call on the light and fill your body, mind, soul and heart with love, as this is the way to an extraordinary life of great joy.

WHITE FEATHER

I have entreated him along with us to watch the minutes of this night, that, if again this apparition come, he may approve our eyes and speak to it.

WILLIAM SHAKESPEARE, HAMLET

Table of Contents

Introduction

Subtle and not so subtle energies surround us. They can be positive or negative, creating safe spaces or, alternatively, frightening us. The positive, wonderful energies can be encouraged and attracted, but so too can the negative, dark energies, which can make us feel confused, frightened, anxious or even physically unwell.

Usually these darker energies are caused by our own emotional issues or blocks; at other times they may be caused by people we interact with daily or, in more severe cases, spirits or people who have passed on may affect the energy signatures around us.

Whatever the cause of the energy, its vibration can have a profound effect on our mood, our health and our personal well-being.

This book will not only help you clear these negative energies from your home and life, but also help you identify the beings of light and give you useful tips to attract and create positive, beautiful energy around yourself, your home, your office and your general environment.

By following the simple, effective exercises, hints and tips in this book, you will not only create a life free from anxiety and fear, but one filled instead with kindness, gratitude, abundance and happiness.

Positive energy is limitless. We just need to know how to tap into and attract the right kind of energetic light into our lives, and how to clear the negative energies which we may have been unknowingly attracting or feeding.

This book is divided into four sections.

Part One: Energy and Auras

In this section we will help you understand the nature and power of energy, for without it life on this planet would not exist. We then turn to your own personal energy, or auric field, and its importance in keeping you healthy and confident.

Part Two: Energies in Your Home and Environment

In this section you will learn how energy around your personal and environmental space works, as well as identify where there may be blockages or issues with the energy you wish to address.

We will also look at the various energetic beings, both positive and negative, which may be interacting in your environment. Only by clearly identifying what types of energetic forces you are dealing with will you be able to effectively clear and remove the unwanted ones.

Part Three: Protecting Yourself from Negative Energies

After you have effectively identified the energies you are dealing with, we will explain how to clear and protect yourself from unwanted energies in your life and home, and also provide simple, effective and clear exercises, techniques and tools to keep yourself safe from the negative forces which you may find around you.

Part Four: Attracting Positive Energies

Here we explore why removing negative energy isn't the only thing we need to do to create safe, sacred and joyful spaces. Attracting positive energy into your energetic space is the true goal. This section provides exercises, tips and tools for bringing positive energies and light beings into your environment to ensure a healthier, happier and more energetic you.

This guide to working with and clearing spiritual energies will help you develop tools for understanding and balancing the darker energies in your life and welcoming in the positive energies of light and love. By doing this, we create more light on our planet, which in turn creates a much more loving and kinder world.

PART
ONE

Energy and Auras

What is Energy?

Have you ever walked into a room and felt immediately comfortable and at home, or met someone and immediately felt uneasy in their presence? When we react like this, we are responding to the energetic fields created around and within spaces, people, environments and objects.

Different types of energy vibrate at different frequencies and create feelings of comfort or disquiet. Sometimes the vibration is so strong, it can physically manifest as illness or disease.

We are all beings of intense energy, which flows through the universe from a divine source. This energy is what keeps life emerging, growing and adapting, and without it there would be no life on this planet. The energy itself is universal and immortal, moving from one form to another, sometimes physical, sometimes invisible.

Your Energy Health Check

Energy is influenced by the two powerful forces in our universe: the light and the dark. Ancient civilisations identified these forces using different symbols, The Sun and the Moon, The Day and the Night, The Yin and the Yang.

It is important to understand that neither force is inherently negative; we need both the light and the dark to keep the world in balance. The key here is balancing these forces and ensuring that the dark never overtakes the light.

As a light worker, I know that the *light energy* is far more powerful, loving and all consuming, as its core essence is divine, unconditional love. *Dark energy*, on the other hand, is fed by fear, doubt, envy, sloth, deceit, cruelty, suspicion, confusion and sometimes pure hatred. People and entities that work, dwell or exist in the dark energies can bring them into your life and pollute your environment through an imbalance of negativity and darkness.

Some of the energies are created by spiritual entities which have either been stuck in the mortal world or who are able to come and aid us in times when we need some extra positive energy. Usually the former are unwanted or negative spiritual entities who create an atmosphere of menace, fear or confusion. Yet many of the spiritual beings with whom I interact are positive, kind and generous spirits who are there to help and guide me towards my best self. Clearing negative energy makes room for these positive entities to come to our aid.

Energy is constantly flowing through the universe and, as it engages with our personal energy fields, the energy of other people, places, thoughts, objects and traumas can get caught in our own fields. Depending on the lightness or darkness of that energy, it can change the vibration of the energy around and in us and create blockages to that flow, or if it is light, loving energy, it can ease our own blockages and create light, frothy, joyous movement.

We are energetic beings and like all natural things we resonate with a specific vibration that can help or hinder the natural energy flows around us. We can feel stuck or blocked by this energy and confused as to what is the cause of this discomfort. Sometimes to make ourselves feel better we try to 'offload' this negative energy through being angry or loud or violent towards others. This does not release the negative energy from our own fields; it simply feeds that negative energy and allows it to expand into the general atmosphere and infect the energy fields of the people around us.

When we are angry, violent, unkind or cruel to others, we increase the negative energy in the world and throw the energetic balance out of whack.

Likewise, if we repress or hold in negative emotions, we continue to grow the dark energies within our own personal energetic fields, leading us to feel unhappy and unwell.

By understanding the different types of energies that work within your environment, you can help positively impact the way that energy engages with you and your own energetic or auric field.

Auric Fields and Auras

Auric field is the term for your own personal life force or life energy. Mediums and people with clairvoyant abilities can often see this energy field in the form of colours, called auras, which halo around the individual.

Different colours can mean different areas of energy flow or blockage in parts of our lives or experiences. By reading the aura and looking at the dominant colours, mediums can see where we may feel unhappiness and identify emotional and energetic blocks, relationship problems and drains on our life force, as well as be able to pinpoint when our energetic selves are strong and resilient.

The Importance of a Strong Auric Field

Your auric field is your psychic defence against energetic and environmental factors. A strong, resilient auric field keeps you feeling healthy, confident, safe and nurtured. If the field is blocked or diminished by negative feelings or outside energies, this can lead to feelings of low self-esteem, meaninglessness, dissatisfaction, unhappiness, regret and depression. In severe cases it can result in physical ailments and diseases.

Even if you cannot see your auric energy, you are always aware of your energetic levels and will notice when things feel a bit 'off'.

Common Aura Types and Colours

Most auras have one dominant colour amidst an array of lesser colours. The dominant colour gives an indication of what kind of energy is interacting with or being created by your energetic field.

Yellow

A *Bright Yellow* aura indicates someone who is playful with a light, joyous energy. They have no trouble connecting to their thoughts and acting on their ideas.

If the *Yellow* is a darker shade or tinged with brown, this can indicate some blockages created by you or others putting too much pressure on you to achieve your goals.

A *more lemony Yellow* indicates a fear of loss and a potential reluctance to trust or commit to a relationship. It may also indicate grief or trust issues around a person.

Orange

Orange is universally a good colour for physical health. If tinged with *Red*, an *Orange* aura can be a sign of strong confidence and a great can-do attitude. Nothing can stop you and everything will go well. However, if tinged with *yellow*, it can indicate that there are blockages around perfectionism.

Red

Red is one of the most powerful colours in an aura and can indicate either positive or negative energies.

Dark Red is a survivor colour. People with this dominant colour are strong and resilient — and often need to be! Their energetic field can be quite defensive and they can seem cold or standoffish.

Brilliant Red is the colour of sexuality, and indicates that you are putting out a strong attraction vibe. It's all about passion, but can also indicate a competitive streak that should be carefully considered. People with this energy are often very attractive and vivacious.

Cloudy Red – if the red colour is cloudy or muddy, this denotes negative energy around you and indicates you are blocked by deep-seated anger that you cannot let go.

Pink

Bright Pink auras are the most loving and respond well to loving heart energy. People with this dominant colour are open and trustworthy and willing to commit to love. They create a sense of trust and people will naturally open up to them.

A *dull, muddy or pale Pink* may indicate that the energy around love is blocked. There may be trust issues or the person is immature in their romantic and intimate efforts.

Blue

A *Blue* aura is all about communication and resonates with the throat chakra and the throat and thyroid.

Royal or *Dark Blue* indicates a highly developed person who has strong energy and a level of maturity and spiritual awareness. This energy provides a sense of authority and leadership. It is the aura of someone you can trust; however, it can also lead to others giving up control to this person and not taking the lead.

Light Blue indicates a serene, trustworthy person. These people have a kind, mothering energy. They are adept at calming highly charged situations, and when they are present the entire energetic fields around them settle.

A *muddied or cloudy Blue* is never a good sign as it indicates blockages or issues around this energy — in this case a block caused by excessive control and/or a fear of the unknown. These people's energy can be domineering and intimidating.

Green

Green auric energy is the colour of the heart chakra and of nature, and is healing.

People with a *Light Green* aura are natural healers and open to love and loving in a universal way. Their energetic signature is soothing and they are often excellent doctors, nurses and natural healers.

Forest Green indicates people with strong affinity with nature and the natural world who are most happy in natural environments. This energy is often fun, spirited and unpredictable, but has a sense of peace and calm.

Green tinged with *Blue* indicates those to whom others will naturally open up and communicate with. They make great counsellors but need to ensure they don't take on other people's negative energy.

Green tinged with *Yellow* auras indicate a creative spirit and great energy around artistic and creative pursuits. This energy is characterised by the bringing forth of great ideas and is often a high, intoxicating energy to be around.

However, if the *Green* is *muddied* or *cloudy*, this indicates blocks around jealousy and resentment towards others. This energy will appear darker and denser and create disquiet and fear.

Purple

Purple is for visionaries and seekers of truth. The darker the colour, the wiser one is. If muddy, there are energetic issues around arrogance and needing to be right.

Purple auric energy is often quite awe-inspiring. These people can be difficult to get to know but there is a feeling around them that something important is going to happen.

Metallic

Golden auras indicate that there are angels and divine entities around a person, protecting and guiding them at that moment. This is light, frothy, joyous energy.

Silver auras indicate spiritual and economic wealth and well-being. This energy will feel light and have a slight buzz to it, like a low twinge of electricity.

Muddy or *clouded* auras in these colours indicate energetic issues with receiving protection or being miserly. People who have trouble sharing or opening up to others will have dark energy signatures in these areas.

White

White auras indicate purity and innocence. They often occur when one is bringing in or manifesting new opportunities or receiving a new spirit guide. This energy is childlike, sweet and gentle.

Rainbow

Rainbow auras explode in a number of bright colours, often radiating out into a sunburst-type pattern. These brightly coloured auras tend to indicate that someone is highly spiritually evolved and connected well with the energetic fields around them and with the spirit world. They are commonly seen around mediums, healers and spiritual leaders. This energy is intoxicating, but can be quite overpowering for people with *White*, *Blue* or *Light Green* auras.

Negative Auric Fields

Any muddiness or cloudiness around an aura indicates issues in that area. However, there are some colours whose presence at all in an auric field can indicate serious issues.

Black

Black auras are the result of holding grudges and refusing to forgive or be grateful. *Black* spots in the aura can also indicate physical ailments and disease in the area of the body around which they appear.

Grey

Although not as serious as *Black* auras, having *Grey* in an auric field indicates blocked energy due to severe trust issues.

Brown

This is the aura of someone who is unable to let go of something that is hurting them, be it a relationship, an attitude, a habit or a situation.

How to Identify Your Aura

Psychic readings and aura photographs

Many psychics and mediums can quickly and easily see a person's aura; however, for most people the colours are not apparent.

You can have an aura read by a trusted psychic or an aura photograph taken using a special machine that allows the colours to appear in a photographic reproduction.

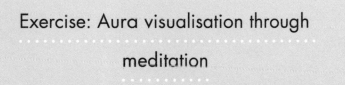

Exercise: Aura visualisation through meditation

There is a useful meditation/visualisation exercise which can help you visualise your own aura:

1. Lie in a quiet space and let your body totally relax by tensing and then releasing each of your muscles starting from your scalp and working your way down to your toes.
2. Once you are totally relaxed, picture yourself in your mind's eye and ask to see your energetic field.

3. Visualise the top of your head and any aura or halo emanating around it.
4. Note the colours you see.

Exercise: Training yourself to see the aura

With practice and an open mind and heart, the pathway of discovery is always open for the student who works with unconditional love and quality and energy of spirit. As you practise seeing these colours in the aura, you will discover a vast number of different shades of varied colours flash in front of your eyes as if by magic. This experience will open up your healing abilities, and the more you practise, it may later on help you as a diagnostic tool in your healing work.

We must always have permission from the client or the client's higher self before commencing any work.

Note: This type of work does not take the place of your own medical doctor.

1. Stand client against a white wall not too brightly lit.
2. Scan auric field with your eyes and hands and notice qualities and characteristics, such as size, shape and strength.
3. Ask the client to slowly count to 40 (with a happy feeling) — this expands the aura.

4. Now look for the white energy around the outside of the body. It will look fuzzy at first, but with practice, on lowering the eyes as if you are looking down, it will become easier to see.

5. Once you can see this energy, continue breathing slowly and feel yourself tuning into the client's energy. Once you have done this, you will see flashes of colour.

6. Work around the head first, then continue down to the shoulders and lower body.

7. Ask the client to think of a happy thought to increase their energy size as they breathe in and out.

8. To decrease the energy field, ask them to think of a sad event; this will make the aura shrink or almost disappear.

9. Often, you will 'see' the outline of their guides, relatives or angels standing next to them. My guide stands on my left side, but for others this may be different. The more you practise, the more you will see.

Healing attachment

Ted cared for his mother while she was dying. She did not want to die and was terrified of leaving her son alone. After she was buried, Ted was fragile and sad for a couple of years. Many thought him depressed — as if his life force had been sucked out of him. He had tried anti-depressants, but they did not work.

He was unemployed and felt something was wrong with him, but did not understand exactly what it was.

When he walked into the healing centre, I could see that his energy was very low as his aura was shrunken and dark and appeared very thin around his body. He also looked pale and tired. As I began to heal him energetically, I could see that he had what I call an attachment in his aura, which turned out to be his mother. Quickly I removed her energy from his aura and sent her straight to the light. Instead of crossing over, she had attached herself to him like a parasite, draining all the energy from his body.

When the healing was over, I told him what I thought was going on in his life and what had happened energetically to him. He understood completely — there had never been a day when he did not think of his mother. After the healing, he was full of energy and looked like a different person. No longer overshadowed by his mother, his eyes were brighter and he felt much better. He told me he was glad that she was gone so he could get on with his own life, which had seemed to just disappear.

PART
TWO

Energies in Your Home and Environment

Types of Energy

Elemental Energies

Elementals are the energies in the natural world, indicated by the four key elements — Fire, Air, Water and Earth.

These energies are ancient, residing in every natural feature of our world. Each elemental energy resonates at a different frequency, and by interacting with and welcoming these energies into our environments we can strengthen our own auric fields.

However, these energies are strong and tend to activate specific feelings, moods and desires that can help us address issues and move forward, or overwhelm us with their power.

As with all things in nature, the key with elemental energy is balance and appropriateness. None of these energies are negative, but too much or too little of a specific elemental energy in your home or your energy field can cause you to feel imbalanced and make poor decisions.

These elemental energies are traditionally visualised through the four key elemental creatures or fairies.

Water

In the natural world water can be gentle and nurturing like a babbling brook, or furious and terrifying like a storm at sea. The power of water lies in its ability to adapt and use gentle power unless more stringent actions are needed.

The element of water is characterised by the *Undines*, graceful, magical winged creatures or water fairies that are found near rivers, lakes, streams and small rocky pools or ponds. Like water itself, Undines can change into any shape or form and they are a symbolic reminder of the need to adapt to one's environment rather than trying to make the environment adapt to you.

On an energetic level, water energy connects us to our emotions and removes emotional blocks. It reminds us that power can be quiet and dignified and persistence can have the same results over time as a flash of furious anger, and often have better relationship outcomes.

If we engage with too much water energy, we can be overly emotional and sensitive to others' opinions and actions, easily offended or too willing to accommodate unfair demands.

Air

Air surrounds us but is invisible and often elusive to capture. Its ethereal nature gives it a highly spiritual connection and links it to the land of thoughts, dreams, imagination and creativity.

Symbolising this elusive nature of the intellect are *Sylphs*, tiny creatures almost invisible to the eye — although they can sometimes appear in physical form, tantalising us as flecks of brilliant light or fluttering creatures too fast to truly be identified. They live in the surrounding ether and are known to be full of ideas and inspiration.

Elemental air energy connects us to our imagination and problem solving. It frees our minds and helps remove worries and concerns that can blinker our thinking. In many ways air energy is incredibly useful, but it can make us a bit too dreamy and unrealistic if we have too much.

If you feel a bit disconnected from reality or that you are living in a dream world, it may be because you need to clear the excess air energy around you and attract some of the other energies to your space.

Fire

Fire energies are strong, fast and unstoppable. They can connect us to our passions and allow us to experience anger, righteousness and fury. They engender creative practical energy and help us feel like we can achieve anything.

The element of fire is characterised by the *Salamander*, a fire spirit known for its resilience and ability to endure, even thrive, in the ravages of flame and heat. Fire energy is useful in helping us deal with issues that need immediate, passionate action and to inject fire and excitement into our lives.

If we are feeling quick to anger, unable to sit still or impatient with others, it could be because we have too much fire energy in our environment and it may need clearing.

Earth

This energy is sensible, centred and considerate. It slows the frenzy around us and allows us to take time to consider options and make good decisions.

This element is symbolised by *Gnomes*, kind, caring fairies who look after the environment and live simple, happy and relaxed lives.

Particularly in this fast-paced age, earth energy can be lacking, but by welcoming it in we can lessen tension and connect with the importance of slowing down and relaxing. It is a softer but still dense energy, which can become muddy and somewhat intractable if overused.

If we feel stuck in a rut or unable to motivate ourselves, it could mean that we are surrounded by too much earth energy and need to clear it.

How to Recognise Elemental Energy

Elemental energy is very strong and tends to be created around natural environments and objects such as plants, water features, fireplaces etc. If you have ever felt extremely relaxed out in the forest, or had great creative ideas while sitting looking at the waves, this is because you are connecting with these wonderful energies.

Residual Energy

Residual energy, or what I like to call a psychic imprint, is what is left behind after a highly emotionally charged event — good or bad.

Everything is made up of energy and energy cannot be destroyed. Usually, when a being's lifetime is over, its energy moves on to the next manifestation, sometimes in a completely different dimension and sometimes as a reincarnated life form. However, occasionally energy is left behind, or imprinted in the natural environment, and that energy is then stored. Because energy must always be active, this stored energy replays the events in which it is trapped over and over again.

Traumatic events like war, suffering, murder, mental or physical abuse and torture can create negative imprints or negative residual energies, while positive residual energies can be caused by happy occasions such as celebrations, important religious or sacred ceremonies, and acts of great kindness.

Some people can tune into these imprints and actually see or experience them; this occurs when we 'see' entities or spirits and engage directly with them. However, residual energies are not the spirits of the people, but rather the residual memories or leftover energies of things that used to be.

The Tower of London has an incredibly varied history, having served as a prison, a zoo, an arsenal, the mint, a royal residence, and the home of William the Conqueror. Today, the fortress is bursting with history and the ghosts of three queens, including Anne Boleyn, and other famous people are often reported being seen or felt. These are examples of residual 'hauntings'.

Even though these experiences feel real and can be unpleasant or unsettling, the energies cannot actually harm you in any physical sense. In fact the energies are usually not ever aware of your existence during their re-enactments.

That does not mean that residual energy cannot affect you, however. If the energy is the residue of a negative experience, this may leave the environment with a negative energetic signature, which reacts with your own auric field — resulting in fear, sickness, or a sense of being energetically drained. Similarly, positive residual energies can give you a sense of unexplained joy, awe or love.

How to Recognise Residual Energy

If there is residual energy in your home, or you encounter it in a workplace or public space, you may experience unexplained waves of nausea or coldness or overwhelming emotions, either good or bad, when in that particular area.

You may find that a particular place causes your hairs to stand on end. In rare cases you may hear voices or even see manifestations of the energy as it plays out its re-enactments. You may also notice a strange, unexplained smell that hangs around, despite all efforts to air it.

If you have negative residual energies in your personal environment, they should be cleared as soon as possible to stop the negativity invading your auric field and transferring the trauma or feelings of the unpleasant experience to you (see sections on clearing negative energies in this book).

Interference Energy

Interference energy is something I learnt about after clearing homes for years as an energy worker and spirit rescuer. I can only describe it as a portal or small tornado vortex, which may be found in homes and other places, creating a spiritual opening to another dimension. If left open it can work *as an open door* to unwelcome guests or spirits from the astral world.

Sometimes we can create interference/negative energy with our negative thoughts, actions and emotions. People suffering from addictions or severe depression may also attract these energetic fields, as can those who engage disrespectfully in the use of witchcraft or the inexperienced use of spiritual tools such as pendulums and ouija boards. It can also be attracted by uncleared residual energy imprinted in a home by previous tenants or a previous traumatic event.

How to Recognise Interference Energy

Having this energy in your house will usually manifest in very unpleasant ways. It can cause hallucinations, chills in the lower legs, sickness, or feelings of dread or paranoia. You may also find that being near a certain area in your home can make you feel dizzy, sick in the stomach or unwell. These portals are often found in hallways or near bathrooms and laundries.

A good indication of a portal is a cold feeling in that area. The open vortex will feel like a subtle gentle breeze which may be slightly cooler than other draughts in the house. Usually the hands are the most sensitive to this energy, which can indicate its presence by a cold or prickling sensation.

Negative Entities

Residual or interference energies can result in unpleasant entities gaining access to your space and occasionally latching onto your own auric field. When this happens, the result can be physically, emotionally and spiritually draining.

There are a number of entities and spiritual energetic beings that you need to identify in order to ensure you clear them should you come into contact.

Lost or Earthbound Spirits

Earthbound or lost spirits are trapped on this plane and unable to cross over after death for a variety of different reasons. Unlike residual energies, this entity has an intelligence and can create physical manifestations in your home.

Earthbound spirits do not understand they are dead, so are often confused, angry or belligerent at your presence in what they consider is their space. They can be very territorial and difficult to move from the space they have decided to claim.

They are unable to create their own ongoing energy fields and need the energy of the living to continue to survive on the physical plane. As a result, they will often attach themselves to a person or group of people and drain their auric fields.

Places such as churches, shopping centres, airports, hospitals, businesses, carparks and train stations are also very attractive to them as these areas offer crowds of people to feed off.

These souls are lost and confused and need to be moved on immediately as they do not belong in this realm.

How to Recognise a Lost or Earthbound Spirit

You may be engaging with earthbound spirits if you find that you feel chronically tired, unwell and physically drained for no apparent reason, or only when you visit a specific place or room.

When earthbound spirits set up house in your environment, the energy will feel completely unbalanced, cold, confusing and strange.

Eight indications that you may be dealing

with an earthbound spirit

1. Your home will feel cold and unpleasant in certain areas, and no matter what you do, the energy will be heavy and unbearable to live with.
2. People living there will feel tired and/or have colds, flus or unexplained illnesses.
3. People in the house or vicinity will feel depressed or stuck in their lives.
4. Fights, arguments or disagreements will become normal.
5. It will be almost impossible to sell or renovate, or make changes to the house, because of the constant delays and arguments.
6. There may be unexplainable or continual problems with electricity switching on and off or water or drainage problems occurring for no obvious reason.
7. There may be unusual sounds, knocks, invisible footsteps, things disappearing, strange smells or constant confusion.
8. You may have goose bumps, chills or a feeling that you are being watched by invisible eyes.

Wandering Spirits

Wandering spirits are earthbound spirits which attach themselves to a specific person and travel with them, rather than staying in the place in which they were first stuck.

Wandering spirits can jump into your car, ride with you in the train, or simply follow someone walking home. They are attracted to people with strong, robust energy fields and light workers such as healers and mediums.

How to Recognise a Wandering Spirit
The symptoms of being plagued by a wandering spirit are similar to those of the earthbound spirit, the main difference being that the spirit may suddenly appear in a previously happy household, rather than be anchored to a specific place.

Poltergeists

Although the word poltergeist comes from the German for 'noisy spirit', a poltergeist is neither a spirit nor a ghost according to paranormal and parapsychology experts. It is, instead, a strong supernatural force or energy.

There is some belief that poltergeists are created by the repressed sexual or negative emotional energy of the people in the place that houses the poltergeist activity. However, the actual cause has long been a subject of debate within paranormal circles.

How to Recognise a Poltergeist
You will definitely know if you have a poltergeist in your home as it will have an energetic feeling similar to a war zone. People in the home will feel watched and physically or psychically attacked.

Each case is different and can be harsher or milder depending on the conditions, but it is always extremely unpleasant to live with or deal with a poltergeist.

This type of dark energy is much denser and very active in murder sites, jails or homes which may have been involved in a horrendous crime. This paranormal activity is not good, but is easy to remove when working with the *light*, as light energy is more powerful than dark. After being detected, it is easily removed by an experienced medium.

Eight indications of poltergeist activity

1. Objects or things may disappear into thin air, then mysteriously reappear in a different spot.
2. Furniture may be moved around, or things may fly through the air right in front of your eyes.
3. Strange pungent smells that are not connected to anything in the room may occur.
4. Electrical appliances may be turned off and on for no apparent reason throughout the day and night.
5. Unexplained noises such as knocks, rapping on walls and footsteps occur, but when you investigate nothing is there.
6. Scratches or injuries with no natural cause appear on your body.
7. You may have a feeling of someone watching you or sitting or sleeping next to you.
8. Something invisible may touch you inappropriately.

Shadow People

Shadow people appear as tall, dark humanoid shapes with an unfriendly, often sinister energy. Shadow people do not like to be identified and usually can only be seen out of the corner of the eye. They will flee if they realise they have been detected.

I have also heard of them appearing to have red eyes and coming in difference shapes and sizes. During my energetic clearing work and spirit rescue, I have often found them hiding under beds or in closets. They are particularly attracted to children, who often refer to them as 'monsters under the bed' or 'the boogie man'.

How to Recognise Shadow People

These dreadful beings generally create a type of dark, sinister, soulless energy which leaves a slimy, nasty feeling in the room. Their energy heightens stress and anxiety, particularly in young children. They are also often responsible for unexplained sleep disturbances and night terrors.

One day I received a phone call from a woman called Suzie, who worked as a doctor in a small practice. She had not long broken up with her fiancé whom she later discovered had been having an affair, so it was no wonder that she sounded very confused and agitated. She said that she was feeling very lonely, fragile and vulnerable and kept repeating that she was desperate for help.

She was referred to me by her cousin whose house I had cleared a few months earlier, so she was aware of the downside of hauntings and spiritual interference in the home and workplace.

According to Suzie, something sinister seemed to be going on in the flat she had just moved into, and she wanted me to come straightaway as she was terrified and too scared to go to bed without the light on. She was convinced she wasn't alone as something or someone kept lying on top of her and scaring the living daylights out of her. Through sobs she said that she would wake up screaming and shaking with fear in the middle of the night and as soon as she put the light on nothing was there, except a weird smell that lingered in her home no matter how much she cleaned it. The other strange thing that happened was that articles of clothing and underwear would be found in odd places. Her cat, too, was out of sorts and kept snarling at nothing.

Suzie told me she was also 'sensitive' and had felt spirit presences in rooms since she was young. She had smoked the flat with sage but, if anything, the strange energy had accelerated.

It seemed to me that she had inherited a resident poltergeist, which I thought might be a male who was behaving badly and trying to scare her, or trying in every way possible to get her attention, perhaps because he was attracted to her. From my experience, poltergeist activity is not usually malevolent, but this spirit was, so I decided to get over there as fast as possible.

As I pulled up outside her building, I called in my spirit team. I had worked on cases like this before, so I wasn't surprised when I started burping repeatedly outside her front door and feeling the usual sickness in my stomach that comes when I sense earth-bound spirits are around. Parts of my body unwittingly act as a barometer for what I call 'stuck energy'.

Walking down the corridor of the very neat flat, I immediately sensed cold static electricity in the air which surrounded and weaved its way around my body. The dense spirit energy seemed to be coming mainly from the bedroom. I stopped suddenly in my tracks when I sensed tremendous waves of thick, wild negative energy, full of sadness, grief and desolation. The despair seemed almost too hard to comprehend and I felt like crying. Calling out who was there, I heard a male voice telling me I had no business being there when suddenly I saw a young man no older than twenty, dressed in bike gear. He said he had lived here since he was knocked off his bike on the highway and that he fancied Suzie, thinking also that she was his girlfriend.

When I relayed the message to Suzie, she nodded and begged me to get rid of it at once. Without further delay, I brought down a light and commanded the amorous earthbound spirit to leave, also asking Suzie to tell the spirit he wasn't welcome.

Within seconds, the spirit and the darkness disappeared and all that was left was a welcoming lightness spread all over the room.

The Psychic Clearing Toolbox

- Organic sage bundle
- Bagua mirror
- Small bell

- Protective amulet
- Programmed crystal: tourmaline, citrine or clear quartz
- Floral essence

Positive Energetic Beings

Just as there are negative energies and spirits that can upset the balance in your environment, there are wonderful positive beings of light who can bring calming, joyous and nurturing energy to you.

Connecting to these spiritual beings can have beneficial effects on your energetic and physical well-being, as well as help you develop or understand your purpose and connect to the meaning of your existence in this life.

Spirit Guides and Spirit Teachers

When working with divine energies, the best teachers that you will have in your development are your own loving guides that stay with us from birth. These loving energetic beings often shared past lives with us and now are with us in spirit or energy form to help guide and protect us.

By being able to identify these energies, you can connect with them to help manifest the positive, practical things you need in your life.

Depending on your needs, you may have spirit guides who help you with all kinds of life lessons and trials. I have a number of wonderful spirit teachers who help me with my medium and spiritual work, including a guide called White Feather whose energy I rely upon to help me when I am studying or teaching, and a guide called

Margaret, who was an ancient herbalist. Her wise, gentle energy is useful for me to help connect to nature and the spirit of the earth.

Meditating is the way that you will connect with these teachers and unique energies. Exercises on how to do this are included in Part Four of this book.

My personal spirit guide/gatekeeper:
White Feather

White Feather, my main guide or gatekeeper, is a gentle Native American whose energy manifests as a voice talking to me in my head. He provides a safe, loving and nurturing energy suitable for study, and is particularly effective for times when I need to learn new things or grapple with clearing old habits or past relationships.

He also helps me with my readings, acting as a guide to the other side and often bringing clients' loved ones over for communication and messages of love. White Feather is the leader of my team of guides, which also includes the spirits of ancient healers, intergalactic beings and cheeky practical jokers.

How to Recognise Your Spirit Guides and Teachers
Spirit guide energy is like that of being in a room with a good friend or confidante. It is nurturing and protective, but also tinged with a

sense of their individual personality. You will get a feel for your spirit guide energy, which can be anything from broody and serious to light and frothy depending on their individual characteristics.

Guides are not interfering energies. They are watchful, waiting for you to draw on their inspiration. You often won't really feel their presence until you directly call on them for help.

As you develop your spirituality, your connection with these spirits will also develop and you will feel their individual energies much more strongly. You will also notice if a spirit guide suddenly leaves or steps back. Don't be alarmed if this happens, as you will be given different guides throughout your life, depending on what you need to achieve in that phase of your existence. Some may work with you for only a short time. When we have learnt the lessons of one guide, they may change or simply stand back, and other guides will then step forward to help us with different areas of our life.

Your main guide, or gatekeeper, will be the one who stays with you throughout your life and their energy will become quite familiar and comforting once you begin to identify it.

Angels

Angel energy asks for nothing, but fills the room with unconditional love and unlimited support. Their presence can often be signalled by a feeling of goose bumps or a dramatic change in the lightness of a room. These are the highest of the spiritual beings and their energies are strong and undeniable.

Angel energy brings in love, light, joyful feelings, strong intuition and inspiration. It usually manifests during our most turbulent periods or in times of great need.

Sometimes our lives can be difficult and hard to bear, and it is during these dark times that angelic energy will help us overcome this. Don't ever be afraid to ask for help from these magnificent beings, as once you connect with this energy you will experience an incredible sense of well-being and deep peace from within, even when in the darkest depths of despair.

My personal angel: Cassandra

Personal angels are integrated with our higher selves; they act as guides and teachers and come in and out of our lives when called. We all have one guardian angel on earth and they are with us always.

My guardian angel, Cassandra, is a beautiful, kind and gentle healing angel. She first revealed herself to me when I started doing volunteer healing work with the Spiritual Church. When I first began channelling her, I thought I must have picked her up when I was a young nurse, as I felt overwhelmed many times in those early days. However, I have since learned that she has always been with me, helping and guiding me through my efforts to help others.

This delightful light being has not only graced me with her presence, but has taught me on so many levels how important it is to honour and love yourself as an eternal soul and to never feel for one minute lesser than others around you.

How to Recognise Angelic Energy

You know when angels are near as they fill your five senses. You may smell sweet perfumed flowers like jasmine or roses, you may hear bells chime or singing, or see tiny flickering lights in your peripheral vision. Angelic energy is always soft, ethereal, subtle and gentle. I always imagine Christmas carols in my mind when angels are around and this sensation always puts a smile on my face, no matter how I am feeling.

You may not instantly recall a time when angelic energy was around you, but try to remember when you were filled with love, kindness and a sense of well-being, even though you were in a difficult situation. This is a moment of being 'touched by an angel'. Connecting with these moments and remembering them can bring your angel closer to you and help you keep that energy in your sacred spaces to keep out negative energies.

Living Spirits

Nobody lives forever. From the moment we are born and have taken our first breath, we are destined to transform back into spirit. Death is not an ending but a transition to another world, another place, another time. From this other realm your loved ones and the people who mattered to you can see and often interact with you by sending messages with their energy through to this world. This is called *proof of survival* and can be one of the greatest tools for healing and helping to ease grief for those of us still in the mortal world.

Mediums and clairvoyants can often tap into these energies to get more specific messages, but the common feeling of having a loved one who has passed still around you is comforting for most people.

How to Recognise Living Spirit Energy

Living spirits use their continuing life force or soul to reach out to us, and we often perceive this energy as visualisations of their living beings, their sounds or voices, and sometimes as shadows, cold spots or feelings of pure love.

Often, they will manifest as signs or symbols that are meaningful to us, such as feathers appearing on our pathway, or in a song playing on the radio that was connected to them in some way. Quite often this spirit will give us signposts or subtle messages to let us know that they are still around, such as appearing in our dreams or creating a certain smell, for example of cigarettes or perfume.

We may feel our loved ones in spirit around us more strongly at certain times, particularly when we are missing them or something reminds us of them. This energetic recall attracts the spirit who wants to comfort us and let us know that they are safe and happy in their new existence. The spirit makes an enormous effort to do this. Because energy is such a fluid, sensitive thing, often we mistake the feeling of them connecting with us as simple nostalgia — but it is so much more than that.

PART

THREE

❋

Protecting Yourself from Negative Energies

Spiritual protection is something everyone should be aware of, regardless of religious beliefs or how spiritually advanced you may think you are or what you think you know. Negativity in any form can damage the aura, create illness, unwarranted fear or depression, attract negative people and situations, cause arguments for no reason and incite anger directed at you. It can also attract negative spirits and entities into your space and attach them to your aura.

The most common way that your energy can be compromised is through self or internalised forces.

These are the things that you do to yourself which can have negative effects on the energy, both in your own auric field and in the space around you. By stopping the flow of energy — by blocking, limiting or storing it — we create stagnant pools of energy, which can, like stagnant water, build up unhealthy elements.

Holding on to, feeding or refusing to acknowledge negative emotions can create toxic environments and physical illness. It can cause conflict within families, neighbourhoods and, if spread across communities, even wars between nations.

Energy's natural state is to flow and move in acts of creation, so if prevented from its natural flow, which is in peace, love and light, it will react by creating pressure or uncomfortable conditions that will force its release. This can manifest in angry outbursts, acts of violence or self-harm, or even cruelty towards others.

Energy is powerful and how we use it matters. Being aware of our emotional energy and how we block or create negative aspects of it can be the difference between a positive, healthy auric field and a dark, unhealthy one.

Once you realise the importance of your auric field on your personal well-being, you will want to ensure it stays as strong and resilient as it can be. To keep it healthy and balanced is more a focus of lifestyle and priorities than any great psychic effort.

Spiritual Cleansing

In its truest form, negative dark energy can cling to you and/or build up in your home, which can cause problems over time. Spiritual cleansing, not just of yourself, but of your home as well, can help to remove this energy.

Experts recommend cleansing your home or work space at least once every three months, but it can be done more often if you find yourself chronically stressed or fatigued or if you have a serious problem.

Psychic protection is an integral tool of spiritual awareness and development. It not only teaches us about the light and dark forces, but also how to work with our own loving guide from the light.

The key idea of psychic protection is that anything that is not from the light needs to go into the light. Once we remove the remnants of negative emotions, or a dark spirit has been cleared by an experienced medium or smoked out over time, the unwanted energy generally does not return.

If you are concerned that there are dark entities or particularly strong negative energies around you, trust your feelings, and do not hesitate to ask for help. Dark energies are real and a menace to us, especially to children. However, they are for the most part easily removed.

If you feel that you are being plagued by particularly strong negative entities or energies, connect with a trusted spiritual clearer or medium.

When engaging with negative energies, it is important to remember that these energies can be particularly 'sticky' and can latch themselves onto your personal auric field rather than be moved on. It is always important, therefore, to protect your own energy whenever engaging in any clearing activity. Luckily, psychic self-protection is very simple and effective.

Below are some helpful exercises and techniques for removing unwanted energies and entities from your home. The best exercise I know for this is the White Light Visualisation.

Using Light Energy for Protection

As energy is often described as light or dark, it is evident that colours and light itself can help you clear and protect you from undesirable energies as well as draw in energies to your sacred and living spaces.

The most universal positive light energy resonates to a white colour — which is actually a combination of all the colours in the spectrum — and so harnesses all the positivity from all the colours, creating a natural balance.

Using white light energy is one of the fundamental ways to create a protective barrier to darker or imbalanced energetic forces.

Based on the power of faith and good intention, the following exercise is the first step in protecting your aura from negative energies. You can use this energy anytime, anywhere. It is especially effective if you find yourself around toxic people — just imagine the white light coming out of your finger and wrapping its beautiful energy around you or your loved ones like a protective cocoon.

Exercise: White light visualisation

You do not need any special tools or even a specific space to perform this exercise. It can be performed quickly and effectively in any situation. It is most effective in a space where you feel particularly vulnerable, such as counselling or practice rooms, your office or work space, even in your car to protect you from traffic accidents!

1. Gently close your eyes and breathe in and out three times, letting all the stress from the day go.
2. Now imagine white energy of pure love pouring in through the top of your head and travelling down into your body. You may begin to feel a warm sensation or a type of tingling on your skin.

3. Direct this energy towards the space, person or object you wish to protect and imagine it surrounding them, like an energetic shield.
4. If you feel the protected space or person is starting to be under attack again, 'top up' this protection by repeating the exercise.

Once you have surrounded yourself in white light, you can activate this protective energy as a tool to protect spaces around you. Or use a similar exercise to protect cleared or positive spaces from being infected by negative energies. You can also use it to protect loved ones, family, pets, homes, cars or anything that needs protection.

I love using this technique before going to sleep. I mentally wrap white, protective light around my bed and room so that nothing can disturb my important night's sleep.

Protective Cloaking

If you want to avoid negative energies coming your way, this wonderful cloaking exercise is extremely effective.

Cloak your energy with a blue light as this can stop negative energy being projected your way. A very good medium told me about this protective exercise; and I use it when I need a break from people and want to avoid those with negative energy. It's almost like a psychic invisibility cloak!

Exercise: Blue light visualisation

Like the White Light Visualisation, you do not need any specific materials to perform this exercise and it can be done anywhere, private or public, where you feel the need to give yourself a little extra protection.

1. Gently close your eyes and breathe in and out three times, letting all the stress from the day go.
2. Now imagine blue light moving down from the universe and cloaking you from the world. You may begin to feel a warm sensation or a type of tingling on your skin.
3. Direct this energy around you like an energetic shield.
4. Occasionally, if you feel the cloak start to dim, 'top up' this protection by repeating the exercise.

Protecting Your Personal Energy Field

Protecting your aura is also protecting yourself, but not in a way that prevents new experiences and opportunities coming in to delight and challenge you.

You want a field that is strong and resilient enough so that you can take risks and enjoy an adventurous life, however you define this, while still allowing you a feeling of safety and emotional comfort.

Fear is not necessarily a bad thing. It can help us avoid things that would do us harm. But when our lives are governed by fear, we often cut ourselves off from new opportunities and relationships.

This forms a blockage in our loving energy and can lead to greater feelings of fear, alienation and abandonment — a vicious cycle of misery as our lives continue to be restricted and less satisfying.

Let go of fear, while understanding that caution is the key to keeping your personal energy flowing well through your auric field.

As with all things, we need a balance of risk-taking and circumspection to advance our life experiences. If we are feeling unsafe or vulnerable, risk-taking can seem even more impossible for us, and energy is more likely to be blocked.

Clearing and Protecting Your Auric Field

If you feel that your energy levels are low, it may be that your auric field has become blocked or clouded with negative energy.

There are a number of quick and easy aura clearing techniques which can be done with little fuss. Once your field is clear, it's equally important to keep it protected so you don't become imbalanced or depleted again.

Bathe to Clear Your Energy

Taking a quick dip in the sea will immediately energise your auric field as the ocean resonates to a drawing energy which helps clear impurities in the energetic fields around it. However, sometimes it's not possible to access a beautiful natural beach, but you can bring the same clearing benefit into your home.

Using Epsom or sea salts in your bath will work just as well to cleanse your aura if you are feeling out of sorts or rundown. As you lie in the water, make sure your body is covered and soak for a good 20 minutes. This process will energise you straight away. I have used it many times over the years and swear by it.

Crystal Clearing and Protection

Crystals resonate to the earth's energy and each has its own auric and energetic fields. As a result, using specific crystals can help you protect, clear and infuse the energy around you.

Protective Crystals

Dark, heavy crystals such as obsidian and onyx are effective in clearing and banishing negative energy as they absorb the energy from the environment before it can affect your aura. To activate these crystals, you can wear them as talismans, carry them in pockets, purses or handbags, or simply place them around your home in areas that feel stuck or negative to clear that energy.

Black Tourmaline

This is the most powerful protection in the crystal world. It not only draws negative energies from around your environment, but actually transforms them into positive light energy.

As a result, it is the perfect crystal to bring into negative situations or places that have harsh, stuck, negative or hostile energies where you either need to stay for a long period or you wish to clear completely.

Black Onyx

This crystal is a protective energy and is said to protect the wearer from psychic attacks and black magic. In an energetic way it is good to wear when you want to protect your aura from those who have the intention to cause you harm and are directing negative, hostile or aggressive energies towards you.

Jet

Jet is an ancient petrified wood and, as such, resonates to a different energetic signature from other mineral-based crystals. Jet is a grounding energy, which can help you to release fears, and is particularly good for clearing and protecting your personal energy field.

Hematite

The beautiful silver shine of this crystal acts as a deflective shield and can be used to protect yourself, your home and personal objects. Attaching a hematite ring or crystal to a pet's collar will give them a protective energy and keep them safe when out and about. Hematite, like the rest of the stones, resonates with the root chakra, but it is particularly useful for giving us a greater sense of personal and spiritual safety and letting go of fear around our very survival.

Smokey Quartz

The lightest of the protective stones, smokey quartz is particularly good for discouraging gossip or drama and is a great crystal to use around difficult workplaces where people may be acting in ways that create mistrust and nastiness.

Smokey quartz can also be used to protect money and valuable items against theft and is great to place in your wallet, purse or near your jewellery items.

Crystals for Positivity

Crystals can also bring in positive energy as well as protect you from negative influences. Most crystals have positive aspects, but the following are particularly bright and happy additions to your home and environment.

Rose Quartz

This crystal resonates with the heart chakra and creates a sense of love and well-being. If placed around the home or carried on the person, it attracts loving energy and can defuse family or relationship difficulties or conflicts.

Turquoise

A sacred stone to indigenous people across the Americas, turquoise is said to open all the chakras and so is a great stone to use in chakra and energetic meditation. It also aids communication and can be used to help create an atmosphere of openness and honest respectful discussion.

Citrine

This yellow stone creates positive vibrations around money and financial security as well as clearing worries around survival issues. It is a good crystal to have with you when there are financial issues around you or if you wish to attract more financial security.

Amethyst

This purple crystal activates our third eye chakra and is useful for creating clarity and seeing beyond a current issue. It opens up creativity and new ways of thinking to get through problems. It is a great crystal to help us clear blocks and conflicts around small problems and to see the bigger picture.

There are many more crystals that can help activate or support positive energies. Finding a crystal that resonates with you is often intuitive, so when choosing a crystal pick up the stone and hold it in your hand. Notice if it has a cold or warm energy. Is it strong and vibrating or stable and grounding? You will be drawn to the right crystal for you and your energetic needs if you approach the stones with an open mind and really experience how they make you feel.

Protecting Your Auric Energy Field Through Chakras

Chakra is the Sanskrit word for 'wheel' as these energetic centres act like cogs or wheels to move energy throughout your body, keeping you in flow and connected to the energies around you. They move and help flow the energy throughout your physical and spiritual system. Just as the chakras regulate and flow energy through the body, they also determine how much divine energy is brought into your system or auric field.

Identifying and Clearing Your Chakras

There are hundreds of small chakras spinning throughout your body, but there are seven main chakras that are specifically responsible for your energetic flow and help create, regulate and repair your auric field.

Your seven chakras are described below.

Crown

Located at the very top of your head, the crown chakra draws the energy from the divine realm and helps connect you to spirit and spirit energy. When the chakra is open, you are able to connect with spiritual beings and can access pure divine energy quickly and effectively. If this energy centre is blocked or sluggish, we can feel like we are spiritually lost. We may find it hard to kickstart our personal energy and have a feeling of depression and isolation from spirit. We may feel we are all alone in our struggles as our connection to our spirit guides and teachers, as well as the divine energy of the universe, is blocked.

Clearing the Crown Chakra

The crown chakra is a great diagnostic for the rest of your chakra system. If it is blocked, this is usually because there is a lack of energetic flow through the other seven chakras. The best way to energise this chakra is by unblocking and energising all of the other chakras and bringing your energetic field into balance.

Third Eye

Located on your forehead between your eyes, this chakra connects to intellectual energy. It is the chakra for wisdom and pure vision, helping clarity of thought. It is also the chakra of psychic ability and clairvoyance. When this chakra is working well, we are mentally energetic, able to solve problems and deal with theoretical and practical situations with clarity. When energy is unable to flow freely through and to this chakra, we can feel despondent and pessimistic about the future. We may lack clarity about our relationships and feel like things are being kept from us. We also often fail to understand and connect to signs and symbols around us, so we miss opportunities which are presented because our intuition is being blocked.

Clearing the Third Eye Chakra

The best way to clear and energise this chakra is to meditate and quiet the noise around you. In a relaxed state you are more open to receiving messages from the psychic realms. There is a chakra/aura cleansing meditation exercise perfect for this (see page 48).

Throat

Located near the larynx, this is the chakra that helps communication flow. When energised, it allows for positive communication of feelings, beliefs and thoughts. It is nourished on the energetic vibration of community, relationships and strong connection between people. When energy is not flowing well to or through this chakra, we are often left feeling voiceless and unheard. If it is full of negative energy, we can often find ourselves interrupting or not listening to others.

Clearing the Throat Chakra

The best way to clear out negative energy from the throat chakra is to speak your truth with kindness, love and compassion. You can practise doing this simply by keeping a journal or diary in which you record your feelings and thoughts. Listening to other points of view and trying to keep an open mind also helps energy flow through this chakra.

Heart

Located in the middle of the chest right at the top of your breastbone, this chakra responds to and flows with loving energy. When working correctly, it allows us to feel safe in our relationships and gives a sense of loving connection with all things. When energy is drained or not flowing freely through this chakra, we tend to feel unhappy in relationships and can be hard-hearted, mean and ungenerous with others. We may also feel undeserving of love.

Clearing the Heart Chakra

Take some time to focus on yourself by giving yourself the unconditional love you deserve. Treating yourself to a massage, a warm bubble bath or even giving yourself a hug will help release any blockages in this chakra. Repeating positive affirmations of self-love, as well as engaging with those you love and who nurture and support you, will also help to energise this part of yourself.

Solar Plexus

Located at the bottom of your ribcage, the solar plexus chakra is the seat of your personal power and identity. It is also the source of your intuition or 'gut feelings'. When energy is flowing well through this chakra, you feel connected to self and able to trust and access your intuition. Self-confidence is high and our sense of purpose or meaning is clear when this chakra is working well. A blocked or sluggish wheel of solar plexus energy, however, can leave us feeling insecure or timid.

Clearing the Solar Plexus Chakra

Believing in oneself will help stimulate this chakra, but we all know that can be difficult when we are feeling down or less than. To help reconnect to your feelings of self-worth make a list of your talents, skills or achievements. Anything you feel proud of. Focus your intent on this list and allow yourself to feel positive about these attributes. If a negative thought or criticism pushes its way in, do not dwell on it; instead, release it by replacing the thought with memories of when your abilities helped you, even in small ways.

Sacral

The sacral chakra is located near your belly button and is the source of your sexual and creative energy. When this chakra is energised, we experience pleasure, particularly with romantic and sexual partners. We enjoy the luxuries of life, good food, fun and sensual delights. If the energy is unbalanced or sluggish, we may experience an addiction to food, drugs or sex. We may also feel creatively blocked or experience intimacy issues with romantic partners.

Clearing the Sacral Chakra

You can give your sacral chakra a quick, effective energy boost and clear the negative energy by doing something creative, or having a fun, meaningful sensual experience with your loving intimate partner.

Root

The root chakra is located at the base of your spine. It is our connection to survival energy as it is our link to the natural world of earthly things and basic needs. When the chakra energy is balanced and flowing well, we feel a sense of emotional well-being, secure with financial matters and a sense that we will be provided for in terms of our survival needs.

A well-balanced root chakra helps us feel grounded and safe. We are also able to draw strong, grounding energy from the earth and connect to nature. When it is blocked, we can feel unattractive, unwanted and anxious, particularly about our survival — whether that be financial, physical or emotional.

Clearing the Root Chakra

As with all the chakras, completing the chakra clearing meditation will help, but on a more specific level acts of kindness, giving to others and volunteering, particularly to causes involved with nature, will help clear the energetic blocks in this chakra. Walking barefoot on the earth and visiting places of natural beauty can also recharge this chakra.

Closing and Protecting Your Chakras

I always remind people to make it a rule to close down all your chakras or energy points if you are going to be engaging with negative spaces or people, as this is a good way to protect yourself from negative forces.

Using Amulets, Talismans and Symbols for Safety

Years ago, a well-known psychic told me she always wore an amulet around her neck for protection.

An amulet is an *object* you always keep with you to protect yourself from bad energy, hexes and curses. They say keeping an amulet with you can weaken the effect of a curse or hex so that it can no longer harm you.

Exercise: Closing your chakras

When you find yourself around negative energy, whether that be unpleasant people, negative entities, or residual or inference energies around your environment, you can protect your own auric field by 'closing up' your chakras.

You can do this anywhere at any time by following the simple steps below.

1. Visualise each chakra in turn, from the crown chakra to the root chakra, as a turning wheel of pulsating energy.
2. As you visualise each chakra, focus on slightly slowing the wheel and dimming the pulsating energy so that it is still shining and moving but in a calmer fashion.
3. Pump white light through each chakra to clear it of any negative energies, creating a stronger, more resilient psychic shield in your aura.

An amulet can be any object that has powerful meaning and is sacred to you. A special piece of jewellery, a shell from your favourite beach, or even a length of ribbon you wore in your hair as a child can all be amulets.

Wear the amulet around your neck or keep it in your pocket at all times for added protection and only take it off when it needs clearing. You will know when it is not working as you will feel less protected. Always trust your instincts.

Some people use a sacred symbol and some a tattoo for protection, believing, according to their faith, that this will keep them safe.

Placing crystals around you or carrying them for protection can also be effective. Natural crystals are basically transmitters of energy — massive clear quartz crystals were used as generators in ancient Atlantis. However, be careful when using just clear quartz for it is a natural amplifier and will increase whatever is around it, and will amplify only negative energy if used in a negative space. Choose one of the more specific protective or positive crystals listed earlier in this book, or choose a crystal that resonates for you if crystals are appealing to you.

The key with using amulets, symbols or talismans is that they are amplifiers of intention and energy and, like crystals, can sometimes energise or activate the wrong energetic forces around you. I have found that they are often only effective for specific people whose energies resonate with that particular object's energies. Finding the right amulet can be a process of trial and error.

I used to wear a cross around my neck, thinking this was a good means of protection, but it was ripped off my neck one day when doing a spirit rescue by an agitated spirit that had hung himself and had no idea he was dead. Probably thinking I was a fool, the mad spirit in all his fury ripped the chain right off my neck and all the tiny beads scattered onto the floor. Horrified, my clients screamed and ran frantically out the door, yelling at the top of their lungs that they were not coming back in until he had finally crossed.

I discovered on that day that amulets don't work for me, although I know they do for other mediums and spirit rescuers. So, if you are going to try out amulets, be willing to experiment with different talismanic objects before relying on them too strongly. If you do want to get a tattoo of a particular symbol or talisman, wear it as a removable object or drawing for a period of time before you make it permanent to ensure it is amplifying the correct energy.

Creating Resilience and Personal Strength

Part of creating strong, healthy energetic flow around you occurs through engaging with and helping others. These exchanges create positive energy and make us feel better in ourselves as part of our role here on Earth is to make the world better for everyone.

How we choose to spend our energy determines how we feel about ourselves and so devoting time and resources to the betterment of others makes the entire energy around us lift and become full of positive light. However, this is only the case if there is an exchange of energy.

If one person is devoting all their time and energy to another and receiving no response or return, then the energy will simply be drained rather than energised. The person giving out their energy will become tired, resentful and often physically unwell, while the person receiving the energy will not feel any better because they are storing that energy in a selfish manner, rather than letting it flow through and cleanse them and giving back refreshed positive energy to the giver or the world in general. Essentially, they will become reliant on others' energy and become a draining presence to be around.

It's an unhappy and unsatisfying situation for everyone, yet many kind, generous souls find themselves in these kinds of relationships.

Creating positive energies and removing the negative is a balancing act of knowing when to remove ourselves and when to engage with those around us. If we are trapped in these kinds of energy exchanges, we need to develop both the personal strength to walk away from toxic people that have no interest in our personal well-being, while also developing the resilience to cope with them until we can safely remove ourselves without letting them compromise our own health and sense of self.

This can be a tough time to manage, so having a strong, resilient personal energy field is important in achieving this balance.

If you are particularly sensitive to energies around you, it's useful to understand that you can't always help others, even if it's in your spiritual contract to be a healer or light bringer. Some people are either not ready or simply unwilling to be helped, and continuing to use your personal energy on them will just drain you and not help them in the slightest.

Learn to gauge the point at which it becomes clear that someone is not going to return or acknowledge the energy you are putting into them, and give yourself permission to let them go and find their own way. If you are meant to help them, then they will return with a better attitude towards you and more open and reciprocal energy. If they do not return, then they are meant to find their own way and path and you have done what you could.

If you feel that the people you are trying to help are trying to do better and are acknowledging your help and nurturing you, then the energy exchange between you will be positive, even if they are still struggling with their own issues. However, if their response is constant criticism, underappreciation of your efforts, blame shifting and lack of self-awareness, then you are wasting your time and energy. This is where strong boundary settings come in. If you have developed a strong, resilient auric field with clear boundaries, you will be able to walk away from them with love and light.

Always trust your intuition and walk your own path. It is important to be true to your own feelings and not make yourself a slave to others' demands and needs. Understand that not all the people you meet are on the same vibration or frequency, even though they may tell you they are. Actions speak louder than words.

In order to be confident enough to keep the energy flowing and moving forward without being paralysed by fear, there are a few things you can do to protect your auric field and open yourself up to negative emotions and release them rather than dwelling on them.

Releasing Negative Thoughts

Our own thought forms can be the biggest obstacles to clearing and maintaining positive energetic space. Among the key elements of creating strong, positive energy fields around us and our environment is to draw positive rather than negative elements into our world.

The Law of Attraction is based on the concept that like attracts like, that positive energy attracts positive energy. If you can train your mind to think positive thoughts, you will attract more positive energy into your life.

What you think, say or feel becomes your reality. Many of us have negative self-identities or self-criticisms, which we have carried since childhood, manifesting in negative energy around us.

When we are engaged with things that we enjoy, the self-critic often is lost or forgotten and we feel happy and contented. But when we are bored, or feeling unhappy or depressed, the mean little self-critic pops up, revealing everything that is wrong with us. This critic has a script that we have written and it is given to us to perform. It's so powerful because we repeat it — over and over — and our belief creates it as a reality.

This belief sabotages our attainment of the joy and sense of well-being that is our right as enlightened souls.

Positive thinking is not about ignoring the more challenging aspects of life; it's about approaching all situations in a positive and productive way.

So, in this exercise, start to become conscious of your negative self-talk so that you can change the script. Don't try to ignore or argue with your critic, as it is trying to tell you what it is you want. Your job is to change the language so that it is positive and affirming. Changing the language can make these criticisms become goals and affirmations, which attract positive energy and help us become our best selves.

Exercise: Changing the script

You will need:
A notebook
A quiet room
Twenty minutes of alone time (this is not something to do with others)
Optional: A fireplace or safe place to burn paper.

1. Divide the pages of your notebook into two columns. On the top of the first column write *Negative Self-Talk*. On the top of the second column write *Positive Affirmations*.
2. Take five minutes to think about all the negative self-talk you hear yourself say or think. Note each of these in the left hand of your notebook in the *Negative Self-Talk* column.

These might include:

I'm too fat, I need to lose weight.

I am useless, nothing goes right.

No-one loves me.

Everyone has always left me.

I am stupid.

Whatever your critic tells you, write it down, and be conscious of it.

3. Once you have done this, go to the right-hand column and change the script of each of these negative comments by turning them into positive versions of the message.

For example:

I'm too fat, I need to lose weight — this focuses on what is wrong with you and something you need to remove. Instead, think about what you would like to attract.

Replace with:

I am a healthy, energetic being and health and well-being is within my grasp. I can become the best version of me by loving who I am.

Energy which was being used to criticise and demean you — and was focused on being fat and blocking your healthy energy — will now be deployed in making you feel healthy and well and focusing on becoming the best version of you.

The weight doesn't matter. You probably aren't as overweight as you think you are, but even if you do have weight issues that are restricting your health, by energising healthy energy you focus on your body's natural ability to balance itself and your ability to make better choices — so the weight issue may resolve itself. More importantly, by removing the focus from your unhappiness about your weight, you remove an emotional block that is preventing you from engaging joyously and happily with this wonderful life you have been blessed with.

Go through and change the script on all your negative self-talk. Example:

Negative Self-talk	Positive Affirmations
I am stupid.	I really want to learn and educate myself.
I am not worthy of love.	I deserve love and to be loved by someone who respects me.
Everyone always leaves me.	I only want relationships that nurture me and in which I feel safe and nourished.
I'm useless — nothing goes right.	It's great how I can persist at things even when they are hard.
I hate my job.	I deserve to be in a job that I am passionate about.

4. Once you have written each negative thought as a positive affirmation or goal, transfer the positive messages into the other pages of your notebook — one on each following page of your book. Be creative with these. Use bright colours to write them and surround them with pictures or symbols that give you joy.

5. Now rip out the first pages with the negative self-talk columns and burn or rip them up with intent to release all of that energy and turn it into positive light energy that is released back into your environment and auric field.

6. Keep the rest of the notebook as your affirmation book and use the affirmations to create posters or signs to put up around your home. Seeing and reading these positive affirmations will give you a burst of positive energy and attract similar positive energy around you.

7. Continue to be aware of your thoughts and attitudes. If you catch yourself thinking something negative, sweep it away and replace it with something positive from your affirmation book — or make up a new affirmation on the spot!

When I let fear go

As a single mother in my early days, I was always fearful of being poor. This fear manifested in odd ways. Although we were all right financially, we had a poverty mentality and never reached a feeling of safety in our financial situation. My daughter used to tell everyone at the time that we ate cat food, which wasn't true! My fear was being transferred to her.

Part of my problem was staying in environments that didn't nurture me because I was fearful of change in case it didn't work out. I lived in fear of the future rather than enjoying the moment and trusting that, if I was nurturing my family and me, we would be okay.

For years I worked at psychic fairs, which are incredibly draining and competitive. One year I contracted whooping cough and was unable to work for four months. At first I was terrified by how I would provide for my family. But we survived, and I realised that this was a reality check from the universe banging me on the head and saying *stop, you need to do the things you really love*. What I was doing was not the only way to look after my family and it was making me physically, emotionally and energetically ill!

Not long after I recovered, I withdrew from all the festivals and started to take time out on weekends to spend time with my husband, go on long nature walks, visit friends and just take my foot off the accelerator.

Things didn't crumble and I gained an opportunity to set up my own psychic and spirit rescue practice. I also took up drumming and music and I determined that every day I would engage in the beauty of the world around me.

This sent the right energy out into the universe and attracted compatible energy. I found that the right people manifested to help me, and opportunities opened up to write books and share my knowledge of the spirit world with others.

Creating Boundaries

Boundaries are basically simple guidelines, rules or limits that a person creates to identify reasonable, safe and permissible ways for other people to behave towards them.

Setting up boundaries in life in our early years is an integral part of our development as a soul. Boundaries form the foundation of our lives — a road map to a good and stress-free life.

When someone, for example a work colleague, boss, friend, family member, spouse or neighbour, behaves in a way that makes us feel uncomfortable, compromised or stressed, it is up to us to respond in the correct way to alert him or her that they have behaved inappropriately. This does not mean verbally or physically attacking them, or being angry with them because these boundaries have been crossed. Rather, it is the act of alerting them to the existence of these boundaries.

Your personal boundaries are unique to you. What is acceptable and unacceptable can vary between people, even for those who are in strong close personal relationships. Others often are not aware of what your boundaries are and do not mean to upset you. Unless you communicate clearly and effectively what is comfortable for you, they may well cross your boundaries without even meaning to.

The key to communicating your boundaries to others is to firstly identify them for yourself. Until you know what is and is not acceptable for you, it is impossible to make this clear to others.

What behaviours make you uneasy or uncomfortable? People telling dirty jokes can upset some people, while others are fine with that as long as they aren't told in front of Granny!

Some are uncomfortable with loud voices, while others enjoy big robust conversations.

Personal Space

Personal boundaries might include our feelings about personal space and how much space we need between ourselves and strangers as opposed to loved ones and intimate partners. Some people require very little personal space, while others get uncomfortable if strangers stand too close to them.

Determine Your Personal Space Needs

Get a sense of your feelings when engaging with strangers. At what point do you feel they are 'invading your space'. At what point do you feel intimidated or uneasy around them? This has to do with proximity. As a general rule, the weaker our auric field, the less proximity we can deal with.

Once you have gauged what your personal space is with strangers, explore how these feelings may change with loved ones, friends or intimate partners. As a general rule, the more we trust someone, the more likely we are to allow them to enter our personal auric field.

Examine Your Boundaries

There is no right and wrong regarding your personal boundaries as they have developed based on your life experiences and thought processes. However, there are instances where your boundaries could be limiting your activities and ability to engage effectively with the world.

It's useful to examine your boundaries and determine where they came from and if they are working for your greater good.

Ask yourself:

Are these boundaries reasonable?

Are they based in a place of love and understanding of yourself and others or fear and apprehension?

If you find that you are keeping your loved ones at arm's length, this may be because you have stored negative feelings regarding trust and intimacy. These feelings may have been created through abandonment or betrayal at some point during your life, and instead of releasing the negative feelings associated with that, you have stored the feelings in your auric field.

These feelings can act like large 'no entry' signs to others, who may find it difficult to connect with you.

While it is wise to have a buffer against people who may not have your interests at heart, it is equally important to connect with loving, kind people who will support and nurture you. To do this, we have to be able to trust others.

So, if you have determined that some of your boundaries are unreasonable, one way to change your energetic field is to do an aura diagnosis and cleanse.

Consider where these negative feelings might be stuck in your auric field. Feelings of abandonment often lodge in our heart chakra and create a muddiness to our green loving energy. Anger at others' betrayal can come from sacral energy and manifest as dark, cloudy red energy, which pushes people away.

We can also have weakened energy around ourselves caused by negative experiences as we tell ourselves that we are not worthy of love or intimacy. This energy attracts predatory people who may exploit this weakness and further add to feelings of unworthiness.

Acknowledge Your Boundaries

Once you have determined what are reasonable and important boundaries for you, formally acknowledge and determine these boundaries. You may like to write them down or affirm them verbally. These boundaries may develop as you experience more in life but should include:

Boundaries around your physical body. Who can and can't touch you and under what circumstances.

Boundaries around your emotional labour. How much of your emotional energy is appropriate to give to others and what kind of emotional exchange do you expect in return. What are your own emotional needs and limitations?

Boundaries around your physical labour. How much of your physical energy can you reasonably be expected to give a partner, a workplace, or family? What are your own physical needs and limitations — have you considered your need for sleep, play, relaxation and personal development?

Boundaries around your moral beliefs. We all have a moral compass, which helps guide us towards what is acceptable. Sometimes in life we have to compromise this moral compass to complete required work or a relationship goal. Compromise is important to creating connections and cohesion in communities and relationships. But you have to determine how flexible you can be around your sense of right and wrong. Moral codes or values and beliefs are a strong part of your energetic self. By overly compromising them, you can create blockages around spiritual and emotional development. Feelings of being lost, hopeless or victimised can be symptoms of a moral compass or set of values that have been abandoned or compromised too much for the sake of others' well-being over your own.

Communicate Your Boundaries

Once you have acknowledged your boundaries to yourself, make sure you let others around you know what is and is not acceptable to you.

Try not to leave this communication until the boundary has been crossed. Have open, loving and considerate conversations about both your own and other people's boundaries wherever possible. Having a clear roadmap will make your relationships stronger and more effective.

As we become more aware of our own boundaries, we become more aware of ourselves — our belief system, opinions, attitudes, past experiences and social learning. Setting boundaries helps us to have a voice and protect ourselves from overbearing and insensitive people who are happy to invade our space, press our buttons for their own benefit or energetically drain us.

Establishing and communicating boundaries can be difficult, but like any other skill it becomes easier with practice.

Tips to help identify and develop your personal boundaries

1. **Always trust your feelings and honour what you know to be real.** Trusting and tuning into your feelings and emotions is the key and open doorway to your own sacred and inner wisdom.

   Feelings of fear, anxiety, resentment, disappointment and anger can indicate that our boundaries have been crossed and we are feeling compromised or not protected in a given situation. Always ask yourself: *why am I feeling these emotions?*

2. **Consider your own behaviour and how you may be reacting in a situation to positively or negatively affect it.** You are the

best judge of what feels *right* and what *does not,* but you must be honest with yourself. There may be times when others' bad behaviour or crossing of your boundaries are caused by you acting unacceptably, particularly if you are being held accountable for unacceptable behaviour. Consider how you react to these situations and when it moves from honest acknowledgement of responsibility to self-punishment, or fair discussion of reasons for your behaviour to defensiveness and inability to listen and acknowledge others.

3. **Have the confidence to speak up and be heard.** Often we make the mistake of being silent or tense, or not having the courage to speak up when bad behaviour occurs. However, if the bad behaviour continues, it is often a good idea to be direct. Learn to give an opinion about what is important to you, as we are all different. For example, 'I don't give you permission to speak to me in this way'. The person may not like it, but when stated gently, they may become aware that they were out of line or being disrespectful.

4. **Don't allow people to think you owe them something or to make you feel guilty.** It is better to speak your peace than feel guilty, drained or taken advantage of. Remember healthy boundaries are a sign of self-respect and self-love.

5. **Get some support.** If you are having problems with boundaries that are important to you, join a group of like-minded people who you can share your interests with. Or seek counselling or other ways to support yourself and your well-being.

6. **Keep a diary of how far you have come.** Often when you read back what you have written earlier, you will see how your life has changed and how confident you have become, simply by setting a few key boundaries — and sticking to them!

7. **Learn to say no.** Saying no can be hard, particularly when it feels easier to agree than risk losing a friendship, relationship or a job. But if you consistently accept poor working conditions or toxic friendships, that is all you will attract. Never be afraid to say no to any situation where you feel you are being compromised. Have the courage to walk away from toxic people, offensive behaviour and people who do not have your best interests at heart.

It may seem daunting, but as you set clear, positive boundaries, anything you lose by refusing unfair treatment will be replaced by more positive, nurturing people and experiences.

Exercise: Cutting the cord to negative people and energies

This exercise is good for cutting off old, worn energy that no longer serves us from people who are no longer in our lives, or mean us harm. It is positive as it helps both parties move on. It can also rid negative energy we may have been carrying towards them and other people who may be tuning into the old, destructive patterning we have been carrying with us. I have tried this myself and have experienced results immediately as the karma or contract is finished.

You will need:

A quiet space where you feel secure and safe.

Optional: A photograph or visual representation of the person you wish to cut ties with.

1. Holding the picture, or visualising the person you wish to cut ties with, visualise a blue figure eight, with gold in the middle. Visualise yourself on one side and the person you wish to cut ties with on the other side.

2. Now imagine ties or old ropes or vines wrapping around you and connecting you to the other person.

3. Note what these ropes look like. What colour is the energy within the ties or ropes? Is this energy thick or thin? How does this energy make you feel?

4. Now imagine yourself with some big, oversized scissors, or a sword or knife. Make it big and cartoony to really give it visual power. Using the scissors, sword or knife, begin cutting through the cords or ties that are connecting you with the other person.

5. When you have done this, cut out the centre of the figure eight and blow the person away into a big pink bubble of love. This is your healing bubble or healing room. No harm can come to anyone, as it is a sacred place of love.

6. As they float away, explain to them why it is not beneficial to have them tied to you. This is not about focusing on their

negative traits but on releasing yourself from any negative effects they may have on you.

7. When you have done this, tell them who you are as a person and how you want to be treated in all your personal relationships.

8. Once you feel satisfied that you have communicated what you need to, tell them you love them and forgive them but the contract you once had is now terminated.

9. With love and blessings, say goodbye and step out of the healing bubble, sending the healing bubble full of green healing light into the source of love. Close down all your chakras.

Replenishing Your Energy

When you are in situations where your energy is being drained and there is no lovely energetic exchange, you are bound to feel low, tired, angry, disappointed or even depressed.

Obviously, the best thing to do is remove yourself from these energy exchanges but sometimes that is not possible, and even when you are able to, you may still need a positive energy booster to help you recover.

Here are some great techniques and exercises to give you a fast, effective energy boost. Many of these can be used repeatedly to keep you resilient in times of great stress or when it is difficult to remove yourself from the draining energy around you.

1. **Surround yourself with uplifting music.** Psychologists,

counsellors and medical practitioners have long reported the positive emotional effects of music to our soul. It can tame a savage beast, make us cry or allow our spirits to soar. The energetic vibration of music is exceptionally powerful, so choose some upbeat, high frequency music to lift up your energy. Avoid blues, ballads or torch songs and choose, instead, music designed for dancing. Gospel music, strong energetic beats and drumming are also effective.

2. **Engage in something creative.** Painting, writing, drawing, pottery and sewing — anything that allows you to release and express creative energy — will make you feel better. Creativity is powerful and it really doesn't matter what you create. The act of creation draws grounding energy from the earth and sends that positive energy out into our environment, cleansing and strengthening our auric field. Drawing pictures on the sand at a beach or building sandcastles can give you the freedom to just create, as the outcome will be swept away by the tide or the wind, so no one will ever see or judge it.

3. **Meditate.** Slowing down your fast-paced lifestyle, opening yourself up to spirit, and giving yourself time to consider and reflect are all positive outcomes of meditation. It also helps you to connect to the bigger spiritual energy around you and draw it down into your auric field. In part four of this book there are some great meditation and visualisation exercises you can use if you don't already have a meditation practice. Meditating for at least 20 minutes a day should be

an integral part of our busy lives as it clears our mind and energy on every level. Just taking 20 minutes out of your busy day to meditate is equivalent to four hours sleep on the theta level, so you will feel full of energy.

4. **Exercise.** Although you may feel this is the last thing you want to do when you are feeling depressed and depleted, exercise is a fantastic way to expel all that negative energy and replace it with new, positive energy. Dancing around a room, going to the gym, walking or running in nature, even just getting those pesky little jobs around the house done, all can all be great ways to pick yourself up and move into a higher, stronger energy. As you walk, dance, run or move, imagine expelling the negative energy out with each breath and drawing light positive energy in with each intake. You'll be amazed at how quickly you will feel rejuvenated.

5. **Spend time in nature.** Nature is the most powerful healing energy available, so connecting to the natural world will refresh and replenish your energy even when you are feeling low. Nature is constantly flowing with energy and tapping into it is as simple as being fully present in the feel of the grass beneath your feet or the breeze across your face. Birds singing in the trees create musical energy, walking in the bush gives you kinetic energy, the plants growing, the trees releasing oxygen into the atmosphere, the tides of the ocean pushing and drawing energy towards and away from the shore, all of this movement keeps energy flowing and will shift your energetic blocks without you ever having to think about it!

6. **Learn to write to express yourself.** Writing down stories or just keeping a journal will help you focus on positive, creative things that invigorate your positive energy while also giving you positive intention. Keeping a diary or journal is a great way to examine your feelings in a safe way and expel negative feelings.

7. **Embrace love.** It is important to surround yourself with loving, supportive relationships. In the modern world it can be difficult to find a loving partner or soul mate, but there are many other nourishing, loving relationships that can heal and restore your energetic field. Loving relationships with family, children, even pets can help energise our heart chakra energy and attract even more love into our lives.

8. **Develop a positive mindset.** Your thoughts and beliefs define your reality. If you look at the world as a negative place, you will have a negative experience of it. Of course there are hard times and the world can be a difficult place, but even in the worst situations there are elements of hope and positivity. By focusing on the good, you attract more of the energies of positivity, so hard times can pass more quickly or become much more bearable. Pessimism, nihilism and negative beliefs create blocks to energy flows and make bad situations worse.

9. **Release things, objects, situations, memories and people that cause you to feel depressed, angry or sad.** While it is important to embrace the positive in all situations, part of

that means also releasing those things that do not nurture or nourish your spirit. Positive thinking is not accepting bad situations and pretending they are good — it is about finding the good people, experiences and elements and following and attracting those. This may mean releasing those things that make us unhappy. Releasing those energies doesn't mean just walking away but also forgiving the people who may have caused you harm. What they have done may not be in your best interests, but they have their own negative energy to deal with. By forgiving and releasing them, you ensure that their negative energy doesn't attach to you, causing resentment and keeping your aura blocked by its continuing effect.

10. **Mix with a variety of people.** Get out and be sociable, even if it can seem a bit daunting. Start with small groups of people you know, or join social clubs offering fun activities. Anything that provides an opportunity to laugh and engage with others will stimulate the energy around you and clear negative blocks.

11. **Find your passion.** Find something you love to do, a passion or goal, and allow yourself dedicated time each week to engage with it. Even if you aren't great at first, it doesn't matter; simply doing something you love will bring loving energy your way. And of course you will get better with practice! The sense of accomplishment and pride in doing something you love will start to fill your auric field, pushing out any feelings of being unfulfilled.

12. **Create a Gratitude List.** If you are feeling unsatisfied or unfulfilled, it may be because you have forgotten to be grateful for the many blessings you enjoy. Lack of gratitude can make our energy fields feel stuck, clogged or sluggish even when, on the face of it, things look to be going well. Make a list of all the things you are grateful for, including gratitude for challenges or hard times, as these have helped build your resilience and ability to cope with difficulties. Also recognise your own internal strength and courage.

Spiritual Healing

Spiritual Healing is about working with illness, dis-ease and dis-harmony from multiple angles. When using spiritual healing to address illness, we focus on bringing harmony and light back to reinforce a person's whole body–heart–mind health. Western medicine focuses on curing people through surgery, pharmaceuticals and other medical interventions. If you have a bacterial infection, Western medicine provides the cure, antibacterial medicine.

Many treatments exist in Western medicine and these treatments mainly focus on curing symptoms. For example, medications are used to treat symptoms of depression and pain. Treatments can be beneficial in acute situations. However, long-term reliance only on treatment can inhibit healing, create dependence on the treatment and even create additional illness and disease. For example, antibacterial medications often create an imbalance in the gut.

Spiritual Healing goes beyond medical treatment. It includes spiritual growth, intellectual expansion, physical cures and other interventions. Healing requires digging deeper into why you got a bacterial infection in the first place and why you have depression or pain. It can also be used to clear entities or parasites from the aura, as they in turn create depression and other mental illnesses.

Meditation and Affirmations for Positive Self-Healing

Often when we take the time to go within, we are able to tap into our own higher self and release our intuition. The soul holds the memories of every lifetime we have lived and has the answers to all problems in life.

Once we learn to tap into this, we also learn about the afterlife and the guides, spiritual helpers and angels.

The best way to connect to our inner selves and create positive energetic healing is to meditate. Sounds easy, but slowing our mind, releasing our stresses rather than holding them and letting them infect the energy around us can be very difficult.

The following exercise is a simple, effective meditation that you can use as a beginner or an adept meditation expert.

Exercise: A simple meditation

To complete this meditation, go to a quiet place in nature that you are drawn to. It should be calming, gentle and protected, free from other people and the stress of daily life.

1. Once you have found the spot, sit somewhere comfortable and feel the gentle sun shining down on your skin, the wind gently blowing your hair and the healing caress of nature's energy all around you.

2. Gradually, as you close your eyes, you will hear all the surrounding sounds around you, but you will begin to slowly let them go.

3. As you begin to slowly breathe in and out, surrendering to nature, you will begin to feel all the tension being released slowly from your body and you will begin to feel completely relaxed.

4. Continue breathing and, with each breath in, feel yourself energised from the nature around you, and with each breath out, slowly release all the tension, all the stress, heaviness and worries you have been carrying in your mind, body and soul.

5. As your awareness increases, feel yourself expanding your energy and surrendering and letting go of everything that no longer serves you or that may have been holding you back in your life.

6. Let go of any trauma, negativity, bad feelings about others or situations, and fear from your mind and cells that no longer serve you.

7. As you do this, slowly begin to open up all your senses and begin to feel, smell, taste and hear everything that is all around you in nature.

8. Feel the warm, gentle caress of the sun on your body, smell the fresh and invigorating air, taste the salt or perfumes in the air and hear the many varied cries of the birds in the sky.

9. As the sounds of nature surround you, feel the wind, trees, water, birds and creatures taking all your worries and problems away.

When you are ready to come back, feel yourself renewed, energised and open to seeing new things in a positive way.

Creating a Safe Space

Smudging and Smoking Your Space

If I am in a room that may have a spirit in it or a bad energy, I sage or smoke out the room with gum leaves and sage from a smudge stick. This is very effective for cleansing a space and getting rid of a menacing spirit that is lingering around as the smoke makes the spirit sick and weakens it. I also have used this smoking technique to cleanse my aura.

If you feel negative energy or you just want to do a quick energy clearing, there is no better way than using a smudge or smoking ritual.

Smoking a space with specific herbs will remove negative energies from anywhere and is a must have for any person dealing with negative entities or wanting to clear bad fortune from their environment.

Sage is the traditional herb used by Native Americans and in its organic form is used in ancient shamanistic rituals to get rid of negative spirits by anaesthetising them. It acts as a fly spray and the offending spirit or spirits can't stand it.

As unwanted spirits live off human energy, this smoking technique acts as a cure or a deterrent. It also clears all negative energy that can linger in spaces in the home. With a couple of applications, the spirits in question will most definitely move on from the astral plane, unless of course there is some kind of unfinished business, karma or reason for them being there in the first place and not moving on to the higher plane in the spirit world.

Exercise: A Smoking Ritual

You will need:

A smudge stick of sage (or one of the other herbs in the list below)

A fireproof glass or ceramic dish

A lighter or matches

A small bowl filled with earth or sand

Optional: A large feather.

1. Place your smudge stick on the fireproof dish and hold the flame of your lighter or matches on a small corner of the stick until it alights.

2. Once the herbs are aflame, blow out the flame until there is nothing alight except a small ember. The smudge stick should be smoking from this ember.

3. Hold the smudge stick over the fireproof dish at all times and carry the stick into the space that needs clearing, having closed up the windows and doors, and wave it in

small circles around the space, letting the smoke waft up and around into the highest and most isolated corners of the room — as this is where negative energy tends to cluster and get stuck.

If you prefer, you can use a large feather to help waft the smoke up and throughout the room, or you can also just use your hand to waft the smoke as you move it through the room.

4. Once you have completely smoked the space, open the windows or doors to let the smoke escape and take with it the energetic parasites and negative energies.

5. Stub the smudge stick out in your bowl of dirt or sand until the ember is completely extinguished and there is no more smoke emanating from the smudging stick. The stick can be used over and over again as needed.

Alternative use

You can use the same technique to clear negative energies and bring good fortune to individuals, pets and objects. Simply wave the smudging stick around the person, pet or object, holding it 10 cm from them, to cleanse and reinvigorate their aura and remove any negative energies.

Smudging Herbs

The most popular herb for smudging is sage, or white sage, which has been used for centuries by shamans across the Americas. Sage smudging sticks are the most commonly available from most stores and psychic fairs. However, there are other herbs that can be used if you do not like or cannot acquire sage.

Lavender

This is a great herb for clearing energies that make sleep or relaxation difficult.

Eucalyptus

The strong, pungent leaves can create a great smoking effect and are used in most indigenous smoking rituals.

Cedar

This sweet-smelling dried wood, which is widely used throughout the Middle East, is one of the most popular smudging options for blessing a new home.

Mugwort

Used traditionally to remove curses and clear negative psychic attacks, it is also fantastic for stimulating vibrant and, some say, prophetic dreams.

Rose

Although less traditional, dried roses can be a fragrant and effective smudging option. They are very good for stimulating love energy and clearing negative emotional blocks around romantic and self-love.

Exercise: Making a smudge stick

Smudging sticks are available from most good spiritual supplies stores, but they are also easy and satisfying to make.

You will need:
Fresh or semi-dried bunches of your preferred herb
A drying rack or suspended line on which to hang your drying herbs
White cotton or twine
A dry airing room.

1. Once you have decided on your herb, ensure it is completely dried, with no moisture left in the plant. Dry them as complete plants, branches or leaves by hanging them up in a cool, dry area, with the head of the plant hanging down. Depending on the plant, the drying process will take 1–3 days.

2. Once they are thoroughly dried, wrap a large handful of the dried leaves or petals tightly together with white cotton or twine so that they are densely packed into a small bundle. The size of a female fist is the minimum size you are looking for.

3. Keep the smudging stick in a dry, cool place until required.

Facilitating Energy Flows

One of the key elements in keeping your energy positive is to keep it flowing through your space. This is the basis of the Feng Shui idea of *Chi*, or moving energy.

Once energy gets stuck or caught in negative areas, it cannot flow effectively through the home. Sometimes this is because the space itself is badly designed, with too many dead ends and areas where energy is stifled or cannot effectively flow out into the bigger atmosphere through doorways or windows. In such cases, any negative energies created by conflicts, stress or negative entities are trapped in the space and often become even stronger and more disruptive than if the energy could flow through freely. Feng Shui is used to help redirect or free the energy in these cases.

The simplest Feng Shui way to redirect energy and stop it catching or getting caught in dead ends is to use mirrors to reflect and direct the energy away from negative areas.

Placing mirrors in dead ends in your home can help direct energy away from the area where it can get stuck and create a bottleneck to the flow. Simply point the mirror away from the closed space and direct it towards an area that has a good flow, such as a hallway or long open room, or direct it towards a doorway or nearby window to allow the energy to 'escape'.

However, sometimes the negative energy is not in your home — you are merely a visitor. Thankfully, you can use a similar technique to shield yourself from negative vibrations. Some people use a type of reflective mirror on their bodies, such as a piece of jewellery or an ornament, to repel any negative energy around or directed at them and reflect it back to where it came.

Exercise: Mirror affirmations

I also like to use a mirror for affirmations. This is a technique that can help you direct energy for healing and positivity directly into your aura.

You will need:

A small hand mirror or compact

A quiet, private space.

1. Hold a small mirror in your hand and say a positive affirmation, staring into the eyes of your reflection.

2. Repeat the affirmation 3–5 times.

3. When you have completed the affirmations, thank your reflection for being so kind and generous and bless the person in the mirror (you).

The key with this exercise is to choose relevant affirmations to direct the positivity your way.

For example, to attract positive or mend current relationships:

I am a beautiful person and I love you. (Do for at least three minutes or until you feel you mean it.)

I deserve the best always.

I am a happily married woman (or man) as I am with my soul mate.

To encourage healing:

> *My body is a powerful miracle that has the ability to heal and care for me. I care for and love my body.*
> *I embody good health and vitality.*

You can use any affirmation to achieve whatever outcome, but remember that an affirmation must be positive and envision the results you want, not focus on the issue or the fear.

Protecting Yourself from Dark Energies

Poltergeists, Spirits and Curses

If you feel as if you have tapped into something unpleasant or picked up some creepy energy which you feel is upsetting, don't keep it a secret — tell someone and do something. You need to use common sense with this and to trust your own intuition and judgement if this is happening to you. As soon as you feel things are not right, like something may have followed you home, or if you feel this in a new place you have moved into, which feels like it has some type of negative energy, give your home or space a good smudging.

I would also suggest a salt bath, or sage yourself in case you have picked up the energy and it is attached to your aura. If this doesn't work and you still feel that something negative is in your space, contact a spirit rescuer — a psychic who specialises in moving spirits into the light.

Removing Earthbound or Wandering Spirits

Negative spirits, as opposed to just an energy block or emotional issue, can be more easily identified because their effect on your life will be far more potent. If you are experiencing issues or setbacks around renovations or a new home, such as unexplained or persistent leaks, cracks, foundation problems, or even rodent or pest infestations, it can indicate that negative spirits are at work. Anything that creates frustrating and unnecessary delays or concerns around your home, such as consistent run-ins with council, problems with tradespeople, break-ins or burglaries, electrical problems, or even the inability to sell a property, can be alleviated by clearing out the negative spirits in your home.

When you are removing earthbound spirits or wandering spirits from your home, you are removing negative, blocked and toxic depressing energy. A simple procedure, like saging or commanding the confused spirit to go, will usually send the unwanted spirit off, removing the negative energy as well.

Here are some other tips for removing or making your home less attractive to negative spirits or energies:

1. Remove any unnecessary clutter as this blocks the natural flow of energy. Clear any clutter, particularly stacked boxes, cluttered desktops, dressing tables and kitchen surfaces, as these can hide or create nests for negative spirits.

2. Give your new home *a good smoke out*, a couple of times, with some dried gum leaves and sage when you first move in to clear any residual negative energy from the last occupants. Also do so after any fights or disagreements in the home

to ensure the bad feelings do not stay caught in your environment.

3. For a really deep energetic clearing, sage or smudge each room twice, working methodically through every room, making sure to open cupboards, drawers and anywhere that negative energy can gather.

4. After you have finished smoking out the whole house, open the windows to let the new energy in. This will create new abundance and allow the old energy to leave.

   After completing a clearing, you should feel a difference straightaway, as the energy in your home becomes lighter and brighter.

   You will also have more clarity around what is blocking or stressing you as things will finally go back to normal and you will no longer have any heaviness in your home because of things going wrong all the time.

5. Once you feel the area is clear, use a singing bowl or small bell and go around the home to encourage the *new* and *positive* energy to come in. The vibration of the music created will encourage higher vibrational energy, which is universally positive.

   Once cleared, the spirit will usually not return. However, if you continue to carry negative energy around you, it is likely you will pick up or attract other negative wandering spirits. In this case, you will need to sage again to clear the energy.

6. You can help prevent negative energies or spirits from re-entering your cleared home by placing a bagua (small Feng Shui mirror) at the front and back entrance to your home.

This deters earthbound spirits by reflecting their energy away from your thresholds. If you are interested in creating positive energy for specific outcomes, you can use techniques from Feng Shui, many of which are outlined in my previous book — *Sacred Space*.

7. Once you feel satisfied with your clearing, light a candle inside the front door, walk around the space, room by room, and talk to your home or space in a loving, compassionate manner. Tell your home how grateful you are for its protection, shelter and love.

If you feel that the spirit is too strong and the general techniques explained in these pages aren't working, get in touch with a spirit medium who can psychically contact the entity and easily remove it.

While waiting for the spirit medium, surround yourself and your family in white light, using the white light technique explained on page 44, as this will protect you from spirits and negative or harmful energy that still may be in your home.

I also recommend keeping a light on as it slows down the problematic spirit.

What is Spirit Rescue?

. . . .

Spirit Rescue is the technique for clearing stuck spirits, energies or entities from homes and environments. These souls are lost and confused and need to be moved on immediately as they make everyone around them miserable. Lost souls or earthbound spirits will often follow people around as they draw energy off our life force.

These days, I am constantly doing spirit rescues, clearings and healings, but there has been one spirit rescue that was most memorable for me — the time I was able to clear an entity that had been haunting me since childhood.

When I was very little, there was a spirit who haunted our home, making the energy dark and dense. I always knew the spirit man lived up in the roof of my parent's laundry because that's where I would often hear footsteps coming from.

My parents' home had a small indoor toilet in the laundry and there was a manhole in the corner of the ceiling, which had a tiny hole in it, the size of an eye. For years, every time I went into the laundry, my skin would crawl as I imagined invisible eyes peering from the small hole in the roof above my head as I sat on the toilet. If I turned my head upwards, I would see the prying eyes. The spirit would also follow me into my bedroom or around the house and stare at me in a frightening, intimidating way. His presence was very strong and my parents often fought or felt unhappy in that house when he was around, but no one seemed to notice him except me.

Although I knew there was something negative and dark living in our laundry, I was too young to understand what to do, so I just tried to avoid him as much as I could and not to think about him.

When I grew up, I moved out of the house and away from those peeping creepy eyes. Then one day when I was visiting my parents, I had to go into the laundry to wash some clothes in the sink. I suddenly felt the old, familiar spirit presence that had tormented me relentlessly during my childhood.

All the hairs on my arms stood upright and I began to feel a cold chill in the room as the temperature dropped. Turning slowly around, I put my psychic protection on and looked up to the roof to see what or who was watching me. The spirit man was standing next to me and, frightened, I demanded to know who he was and what he was in doing in my parents' house.

At first he said nothing. He just stood in front of me, confused and frightened, as if he didn't understand what was going on. He appeared the same size as me but was very fuzzy — just as I remembered him.

The spirit man was very confused and told me telepathically that he didn't know where he was or what was going on for that matter. He did not realise that he was dead, instead believing that he had always lived in our roof. He didn't know who the other people living in the house were, though he remembered me as I had seemed to notice him when I was a kid and none of the others did.

Despite my fear, he wasn't an angry spirit and seemed more afraid of me than I was of him. He knew I could see and hear him, and I sensed he had known me from my childhood. He was so confused; he couldn't even give me his name.

Where he came from and why he had not crossed over when he died, I will never know, as I was not given this information. It doesn't really matter. Sometimes spirit just works that way. I don't have all the answers, and it will always remain a mystery.

I can only speculate that he might have lived in my parents' house before he died and, instead of crossing over, came back to the house.

Realising that all my childhood fear had been for nothing, I gently told him that it was time for him to cross over and reassured him that everything would soon be okay.

Calling on my spirit helpers, I asked Great Spirit and my spirit team to open up a portal of love and light so I could send him home, which was back to spirit where he belonged. Next, I lovingly told him to open his eyes and go into the light. I told him he was dead and it was time to go *home* where his loved ones were waiting for him in the spirit world.

Once he had crossed, the energy in my parents' house lightened considerably and everyone seemed much happier and healthier.

Using Ouija Boards and Spirit Communication

One guaranteed way of bringing negative energies and entities into your home is using Ouija boards or other tools of spirit communication in a way that is not respectful or careful.

While the use of these tools can be effective for mediums and those trained in their use, they are a common cause of interference energy and dark energy portals.

If they have been used in your home or office, then clearing the space is essential. But the best advice is to avoid using these tools unless you are a sensitive or medium with experience so that you understand how to do so safely.

Protecting Psychic Children

Psychic ability is what I can only describe as an odd radio frequency transmission straight into the spirit world. When I open up this energy, I am able to receive clear and concise answers to anything I want, usually for friends, clients and myself. This ability has always been with me, even as a small child, and looking back at my own childhood, life would certainly have been easier if I had known why this was happening and had been supported and assisted in my development rather than treated as weird, strange or difficult.

Some children have extraordinary abilities and this is becoming even more common. I have met children who can talk to trees and animals or see colours around people's energy fields or auras. Many of these gifts are also brought in from past lives and these children often 'remember things' from a time long before they were born.

Psychic children have chosen to be part of our new world and to be the new leaders on this planet. These enlightened souls have their gifts for a reason and, as part of the spiritual contract they signed up for in spirit, are here with a unique purpose of creating change, manifesting blessings and helping restore the energy of love and peace on the planet.

Many also have a profound ability to bring healing to others — spiritually, mentally and physically. They may share messages from the other side, or simply complete this work through their vibration of love, light, and joyful presence in the moment.

My gift and aim as a medium is to help as many people as I can. I have a great love of helping children, especially those souls that are very important energetic beings.

How to Recognise a Psychic Child

As we go through changes on the planet, more and more children who are different are being born. Some of these children have, what we call, Rainbow, Indigo and Crystal energies.

Rainbow children: These children are entirely fearless and are already at their spiritual peak. They are also known as 'Star children'. They are incredibly advanced in understanding and have strong spiritual and kinetic energies around them.

Crystal children: These deeply gifted individuals have deep soulful eyes and a soft calling energy. I have seen many of these children and one of my daughters is one. She is extremely sensitive and very intuitive and she did not speak until she was three years old.

Indigo children: Being born an Indigo child myself, I understand how it feels to be different. Indigo children are usually old souls and very driven and stubborn, and seem to answer to a higher calling. They also have a purple halo around the top of their heads in their aura. Indigo children often grow up to be powerful psychics and mediums.

To identify if your child may have psychic abilities or resonate to higher energetic frequencies, consider the following traits common to many psychic children:

- Highly sensitive, physically and emotionally, to other people, places or things
- Have a heightened awareness and intelligence, an incredible imagination and are generally very creative in a variety of ways
- Can be demanding and challenging
- Are prone to nightmares or vivid dreams that seem real
- Speak about things they would not normally be expected to

understand or know about, including specific details about people they do not know, deceased loved ones, or past lives

- Are described as not having a filter
- May suffer anxiety or have headaches
- Generally feel like they do not fit in and are often bullied by other children who describe them as weird
- Are able to see auras and are generally very inquisitive.

Any child who is able to 'see spirit' or sense the world in different ways is bringing us gifts from the other world and past lives to help us understand our own spiritual contracts.

These children are so in touch with their own power if they are shown how to use it. Often they understand their abilities but are left feeling vulnerable and powerless because of fear of others, and are prone to anxiety.

I have heard many psychic children talk of things that they could not possibly know anything about and this often confuses and frightens the adults around them.

When I was small, I always talked about living in a cold country and having to make a fire. My mother never understood what I was talking about and would often try to dissuade me, claiming this was just my imagination. However, years later, as an adult, I was drawn to Norway, and when I finally was able to live there it felt like home. I was able to learn and speak the language fluently within six weeks. It was clear to me that this was the cold country I had been describing when I was a child.

Ways to Protect and Encourage a Psychic Child

Children with highly developed psychic sensitivities can be a magnet for attracting other energies, both good and bad. Often they are not aware of who or what they are engaging with, and as a parent or guardian of a psychic child, it is important to protect them without discouraging their unique and profound gifts.

The following are some steps you can take to protect and nurture your psychic children:

1. Learn to listen to what they have to say and to believe them, even though it may seem extraordinary. In their eyes, what they see is real and they are usually much safer and more secure if they can openly discuss with you what is happening to them. By understanding what your child is experiencing, you can help them to harness their abilities and focus them in positive directions.

2. If they are having visitations in the night, encourage them to have a night light on. This will generally deter any spirit that may be around, as spirits generally like to creep around in the dark.

3. Teach them the White Light Visualisation (see page 44), so they can surround themselves with positive energy and deter any negative attachments that may be drawn to them.

4. Watch their diet for hidden sugars as these are not helpful for their general well-being. Too much sugar in the blood will make them even more overactive than what they are already and it will be difficult for them to concentrate or focus, leading to feelings of irritation and imbalance.

5. Teach them the art of meditation. This can be done via CD or video. You can also enrol them in a meditation class for young children so they can learn to listen to their own guides and inner voice.

6. Use crystals like rose quartz to create a positive energetic field around them, particularly in their bedroom. The protective crystals outlined on pages 48 to 50 of this book are also useful to deter negative energies that will be attracted to your sensitive child. If possible, allow your child to choose their own special crystals as they will have a strong ability to choose exactly the right energetic crystals for them.

7. Encourage them to enrol in a martial art, yoga or Tai Chi as this will centre and ground their energies while giving them a good outlet for the huge energetic build-up that is a part of being a psychic child.

Growing up as a Psychic Child

Like many natural mediums, my paranormal experiences began happening to me from a very young age. Dead people, or *living spirits*, were visiting me and telling me things before I could even talk. As I grew older, I started to understand what I was experiencing. When I told Mum about one particular visitor, she said that person had died a long time ago.

Unfortunately, nobody else seemed to be able to see or hear these spirits, and I just learnt to pretend it wasn't happening and, more importantly, not to say anything about it in case I got into trouble.

My spiritual teachers have always told me my beloved Spirit will look after me when I have an open heart and do the work, and that Spirit will also never give me anything I can't handle. Overall, this is true, but it's also true that being a psychic kid was not easy!

Gradually I learnt how to turn off the psychic radio by immersing myself in books. When I occupied my restless mind with fascinating stories of heroes, adventure, magic and intrigue, the very busy spirit community that I was forever surrounded by simply faded back into their dimension. I knew the spirits were still there but they were no longer getting my full attention.

Over the years, spirits have made life difficult for me. I am still extremely sensitive to almost every type of energy around me. I still wonder why I was born into a family who gave me no support for my gifts. Of course, it would have been a whole lot easier if they had been like me, but I believe now that growing up with these experiences was all part of the spiritual contract I signed up to while in the spirit world.

Growing up as a child with spirit visitors was tough, but it has made me who I am today. Now I make sure I offer as much support and help to other psychic children as I can.

PART
FOUR

✳

Attracting Positive Energies

While it is important to clear the energetic fields around you of negative energy, it is equally important to intentionally attract positive energies to fill the void. The key to attracting positive energy is similar to that of all universal forces: like attracts like and intention fuels outcome. If you are focused on dark, negative emotions or experiences, that is what you will attract. However, even if you are in a difficult or challenging period of your life, you can still bring positive light energy back into your aura and energetic field by focusing on the good in your life and the world in general.

Fill Your Space with Positive Energy

Whenever I am feeling sad, down or at breaking point, I always try to have a good laugh. I might call a friend to natter, hang out with my loved ones, see a funny movie, or read a humorous book. Spending time with people you love or doing things that bring you joy will immediately change the energetic signatures around you.

Negative energy takes its power from negative emotions, and its opposite, positive energy, has the power to weaken them. Therefore, laughter really is the best medicine because you can use it quite effectively against any type of negative energy, including when you feel under psychic attack or curse.

You don't need a ritual or a spell, just your own well of positive energy. When you feel the effects of negative energy around you, think of something funny and laugh. Or focus entirely on a funny video or book and let yourself fully enjoy how it makes you feel.

When you're confronted by a person you suspect is directing negative energy towards you, smile and be friendly, because acting as if you are not affected in anyway will make them think they have no hold over you whatsoever.

If you are not able to cope with what is going on in your life, go and see a spiritual healer, hypnotherapist or someone who is trained in energy as a light worker as they can clear negative energy without any problems.

Affirmations

One of the most important keys for creating positive energy is through eliminating insecurities and establishing a habit of self-love. The best way to do this is through the use of affirmations. These really work because they raise your vibration, especially when said in front of a mirror where you express them to your eyes — the windows to the soul.

Affirmations are known as *food for the soul* and just expressing loving words loudly and clearly reinstates who we want to be in our own eyes. Through affirmations we can think ourselves healthier, have a healthy and happy love life, improve toxic relationships by having the confidence to walk away, feel confident and accomplish everything we ever dreamed about.

Here are a few affirmations that may work for you:

> *I am a beautiful person and I love you.*
> *I am now ready to have a great life, with exciting possibilities.*
> *Every day in every way, I am loved unconditionally, supported always and feel safe.*
> *I deserve the best in my relationships and only have the right people in my life.*
> *I always find myself in the right place at the right time to receive golden opportunities.*
> *Every day in every way my life gets easier and more comfortable and nothing is a problem.*
> *I am always grateful for the blessings I have in my life. I am truly blessed.*
> *The world is a happy place and I am elated to have so much abundance I can share with others I love.*

If used every day, these simple affirmations will become part of your mindset and can never be taken from you, and they will open a new reality you only once dreamed about.

Bach Flower Remedies for Positivity and Healing

Edward Bach was a doctor in Birmingham who later became a well-respected surgeon. He was also an amazing healer and had an understanding of the emotions of the people he treated.

After working for many years in private practice and as a medic during World War II, Bach grew increasingly frustrated with the focus of modern medicine on illness or the problem and wanted to develop a more holistic approach to treating his patients which took into account the effect of their mood and the energies around them.

He was soon working with homoeopathic medicine at the Royal London Homoeopathic Hospital where he started to develop a system of remedies using the energetic and healing properties of the natural world.

Although quite revolutionary at the time, Bach's flower remedies have become one of the most popular and effective ways to deal with the energetic and emotional issues that underlie many modern ailments.

These powerful flower essences are based on the idea that natural energies, or essences, of the mineral and plant kingdoms can be distilled and harnessed to change our own energetic signatures and bring us more in tune with our natural state of balance.

Many of the remedies are taken orally to ease specific medical symptoms, but Bach flower remedies can also be effective in clearing and energising the spaces we inhabit.

One of the most effective Bach remedies for space or energetic clearing is Crab Apple essence.

According to Dr Bach, the crab apple is a strong energetic force for removing a sense of impurity. He described it in his many teachings like this:

[Crab apple] is for those who feel as if they have something not quite clean in themselves. They are anxious to be free from one particular thing, which is greatest in their minds and which seems so essential to them that it should be cured.

You can use Crab Apple essence to give a deep spiritual cleanse to objects or items you feel are holding on to or attracting negative energies. It is also a super-powered clearing agent for cleansing crystals to ensure they are working to their full potential.

Exercise: Crab Apple Essence cleansing

You will need:
> *Your crystals or the item you wish to clear*
> *A small bowl*
> *A small water jug*
> *Sea salt*
> *Purified water*
> *A bottle of Crab Apple Bach Flower Remedy.*

1. After cleaning and rinsing your bowl, place the items you wish to cleanse in the dry bowl. If cleansing more than one object at a time, make sure your bowl is big enough so that you can spread the objects out so they are not touching each other at any point.
2. Sprinkle a few pinches of sea salt into the jug with the purified water.
3. Pour the water and salt mixture into the bowl so that it just submerges the item or items.
4. Add 8 to 10 drops of Crab Apple flower essence to your bowl of water.
5. Leave the bowl out in the sunlight for 8 hours or more.

The Twelve Healers

Although there are many flower remedies that can be used for a variety of energetic and spiritual purposes, there are 12 specific essences that are regarded as the most effective for spiritual and energetic healing.

As with all flower remedies, these can be taken internally in a brandy or water solution to help clear your personal auric field, but all of the flowers and plants that form these essences can also be brought into your home to heal the space itself of energetic blocks or issues.

Agrimony

The Agrimony flower helps those who hide their pain or ailments behind a cheerful facade in order not to burden others with their suffering.

While positive thought processes are great for shifting negative energies, ignoring or avoiding real pain or suffering prevents honest and clear communication of these struggles and can often leave the atmosphere full of unspoken anger, resentment and pain. Bathing in or burning Agrimony flower essence can help open an energetic connection to true acceptance of such conditions and allow subsequent transformation.

Centaury

The flower essence for those who cannot say no! If we cannot say no to others, then boundaries are broken and we gain no true value of self. Centaury flower essence strengthens the energetic vibrations that allow us to feel our life, choices and boundaries are real, important and deserve respect.

Cerato

Cerato flower essence helps clear the energy of those who do not trust their own instincts. It helps us rely less on the advice of others and listen as intently to our own inner voice. While seeking advice is often useful, it creates emotional and spiritual blocks when it is used as a crutch to prevent us from acknowledging or listening to our own inner wisdom and spiritual understanding.

Chicory

If your home is filled with the energy of self-pity and lack of appreciation, Chicory flower essence can help you clear this by changing the energetic vibration of needing reassurance or playing the martyr to loving energy pathways directed outward with generosity and consideration. It is particularly useful for children who have a pattern of selfish or attention-seeking behaviour.

Clematis

If the energy around you is dreamy and lethargic and needs an energetic boost for action, Clematis can help channel this lovely dreamy energy into a strength of purpose and goal-orientated focus. It is particularly effective for those whose inner life of creativity and connection to spirit, dreams and visualisations is strong but have trouble manifesting these into any real outcomes in the physical world.

Gentian

Those in need of Gentian flower essence are easily discouraged when setbacks occur. They live in a constant state of believing that nothing will ever go right and often doubt the possibility of their own healing. Gentian brings a more positive energy to our futures and personal health and prevents us from becoming disheartened or overwhelmed when things aren't going as planned. It is a great essence to use if you are in a career or profession and facing rejection or high competition for your role as it creates resilience and a sense of achievement even when faced with what may look on the surface to be a negative outcome.

Impatiens

Unsurprisingly, this is the healing essence for those affected by high levels of impatience — individuals who are often thinking about or pushing far ahead of the present moment, and thus missing the beauty around them in the present. An individual needing Impatiens can often feel truly and profoundly lonely as they are never in step with those around them, always rushing to the next person or thing rather than enjoying the company of those who are with them at the moment.

Mimulus

When faced with overwhelming fears of the everyday world or feeling hypersensitive to everyday events, our energetic field can be charged with highly negative energetic vibrations. Mimulus helps us to gain a sense of proportion and courage to face these everyday obstacles and replace fear energy with the joy and excitement of a life lived well.

Rock Rose

While Mimilus deals with everyday fears that make us feel timid or shy, rock rose helps us overcome more profound fear or terror. This potent essence is specifically for those who are truly in need of energetic rescue as it helps clear the remnants of exceptionally traumatic events or experiences.

Scleranthus

Those battling with indecision, confusion or procrastination would do well to bring some scleranthus into their environment. Inability to decide on the best course of action or constantly putting off important decisions leaves the aura and environmental energy drained and exhausted, often manifesting as personal lethargy and irritation. Scleranthus can help remove this block by assisting in defining the problem, summoning the strength to form an inner resolve and committing to a decision or to undertake a course of action. This will allow a great release of energy, which will literally feel like a weight being lifted from your shoulders.

Vervain

Vervain is the balancing essence, useful in bringing a sense of balance to most situations. The energy in Vervain is strong and can be used to address issues of extremes, particularly around those who are stubbornly inflexible. Essentially this energy will help repair the mind–body connection and bring grounding and earthly balance, allowing even the most strong-willed person to find the flexibility necessary for them to move forward.

Water Violet

This essence helps open the hearts of those who are avoiding deep bonds with friends and family. Whether due to childhood experiences, past lives, or difficult relationships in adulthood, we often create barriers around our hearts, which can prevent us truly connecting with others. Although those suffering from this lack of connection can seem to be functioning perfectly well, their lack of deep love and companionship stifles their growth and creates emotional blocks around the heart chakra. The gentle energy of Water Violet is a calming, soothing vibration that can open this most delicate of energy centres.

My Own Experience with Flower Essences —

Cherry Plum

Many years ago, after a particularly difficult period in my life, I was diagnosed with a complete nervous breakdown. I was stuck in a toxic relationship and felt like there was no way out. This was manifesting as chronic illness and pain, and several trips to doctors and specialists achieved nothing but further frustration.

Eventually, I consulted a spiritual healer, who instantly understood that my energetic signature was blocked and caught in a vicious cycle of negativity — a feeling that I had lost control and could not regain it.

I recognised the person he was describing, as I had been feeling lost and unable to cope, telling myself over and over again that nothing would change, that I was trapped and I was never going to get better.

The remedy he prescribed was the wonderful Bach flower essence, Cherry Plum, which is designed for those who fear their mind is deteriorating and that they will no longer be able to cope with life.

Cherry Plum essence breaks the cycle of negativity. It helps you to acknowledge that you can cope even though you think you may not.

Within 24 hours of taking the remedy, I was back to my normal self, with a belief in my own capacities and a clear plan of how to rectify my life. By making clear decisions about my life and where I was going, I was soon able to go back to work, leave the relationship and move forward.

Connecting to Positive Energies

In part one of this book, you were introduced to some of the wonderful positive entities that can bring love and joy to your energetic field. While it's great being able to know they exist, it is even better being able to connect with them and draw them into your environment for additional protection and good fortune.

Angels, spirit guides and elementals from the fairy realm are all willing to engage with you if you learn how to communicate energetically with them.

Crystals to Help You Connect to Positive Energies

I love to sleep with different crystals by my bed. I also wear them close to my body at all times. If not worn as jewellery, you can store them in your clothes or carry them in a soft little pouch. They may also be placed on your altar or used in meditation.

The following crystals are particularly useful to help unlock your past life memories, which may indicate some energetic blocks you may still be carrying from your previous lifetimes.

Blue Apatite

This is a stone of psychic activation and cosmic connection that makes you clearer and more tuned in. It helps you tune into your Akashic records — the energetic record of all our lives in all dimensions. It can clear chakras, emotional states, patterns and psychic debris in the aura. It opens the senses to clairvoyance, clairaudience, clairsentience and claircognizance, as well as channelling and telepathy.

It also helps you connect to extraterrestrial (ET) energies such as the Blue Beings, Andromeda, Arcturus, Pleiades, Sirius and Vega. When working with these energies, it is important to work with your highest intention for healing on all levels. Please note, when inviting ET connection, it is best to call in only the parts of your own soul that are positively oriented extraterrestrials, rather than sending out a general call to all aliens out there. As with all forces in the universe, there are also dark ETs that are here not to serve mankind, but to cause malice and destruction.

Moldavite

This cosmic gemstone is known as the crystal from the stars. This stone is the result of a meteorite crash that occurred millions of years ago. It brings in high frequencies of light that activate and clear all chakras and the energy field. It also brings in new connections, bright opportunities and a positive flow that is true to your mission here on earth, if you choose to take it on. It heightens all your senses to a higher frequency and helps you remember your star origins.

Stellar Beam Calcite

This healing stone represents the manifestation of the new reality. It helps with transformation, galactic energies and better understanding of belonging to the earth's plane. It is also a vehicle for accessing the stars and actualising higher dimensional living. It is a good crystal for manifesting and clearing all types of negative energy, including attachments.

Labradorite

This is what I call the *psychic's stone*, as it is popular amongst most healers who work in the field. It is a truly beautiful crystal that exhibits flashes of iridescent peacock colours when held in the light. When used or worn, it can shift and align your energy to a higher consciousness. It can also align you to the following qualities: clairvoyance, telepathy, astral travel, prophecy, psychic readings, Akashic records access, past life recall, and communication with guides and spirits. It is believed to have extraterrestrial origin. Labradorite grounds the spiritual and stellar energy in your bio-system so that you can use it in the most tangible ways.

ET Crystal

This is a quartz crystal that has multiple points, or terminations, on one end. It can help you communicate with ET consciousness and with the integration of your other lifetimes.

Meditation to Connect to Your Guides

One way to ensure you feel protected and secure in your space is to bring in the protective, loving energy of your personal spirit guide.

As mentioned in the first part of this book, we have a number of different guides across our lifetimes depending on what energy we are dealing with. However, our Guardian, or main spirit guide, stays with us from our first breath until our last. It is this energy that can nurture us in times of difficulty as well as help us work out the best way forward in life.

Connection with this guide is available to anyone who asks. This energy tends to be non-interfering unless directly asked to intervene in times of intense danger.

Asking for this connection, however, is simple through a gentle, effective meditation. If you practise this connection with patience and love on a regular basis, you will find a strengthened connection to your higher self, or soul's energy, and a dramatic positive shift in the energies around you. It will also connect you to your own loving guide, who is always with you from birth until death.

Exercise: Spirit guide meditation

You will need:
> A quiet place to meditate
> Optional: A pillow or chair to sit on.

1. Find a quiet place where you will not be disturbed. Sit in a comfortable position and breathe deeply until you feel your body relaxing. Exhale any tension from the day and any negative thoughts, emotions or mindsets you may have created in your mind.

2. Imagine your mind is a brand-new blackboard and you are now dusting it off, creating a clean space, full of fresh ideas, hopes and inspirations. Visualise yourself sitting in a white pyramid filled with the golden holy light of protection and love.

3. Visualise energy in the form of white light coming down from the top of your head and moving slowly down into your heart chakra, filling your whole body with love. Feel this energy and, with your own aura, expand it as far as you can take it.

4. Now bring it back and take it down to the rest of your body and centre it into the Earth.

5. Silently count to 10, and then imagine you are in a beautiful garden. Look around you and imagine all the details. Hear the breeze sighing through the trees, smell the wafting fragrance of beautiful blooms, feel the soft green grass under your feet and see the blue sky above.

6. Feel yourself relaxing more and more as you visualise what your garden looks like. Once you have created your inner garden of tranquility, call in your own loving guide from the light and feel the presence of eternal love.

7. Ask whatever entity appears if it is from the light. If it says no, send if off to the light and continue asking your guide to step forward until you feel you have connected to your true guide from the light.

8. When you have connected, ask for healing or any information you may need to help you on your journey. Take your time and fill your soul with gratitude, as you are now able to connect with your soul's energy and your inner power whenever you need to.

9. When you are finished, come back into the room and imagine the golden triangle being placed around your own energy field. Don't forget to offer gratitude to spirit for everything you have in your life.

Connecting with Your Passed Loved Ones

It takes a lot of effort on the spirit's part to get a message of love across, even though, more often than not, they will leave plenty of signs. Here are a few suggestions to make the process a whole lot easier.

- Believe this is possible no matter how hard you try to make yourself a sceptic. With an open mind anything is possible.

- Pray, as this is a powerful force and a good way of calling loved ones to come closer to give you a signpost from spirit that they are around. Miracles do occur all the time, on a daily basis.

- Communicate with loved ones through dreams, as spirit will often give us messages while we are sleeping.

- Talk to a picture of your loved one. This is something I recommend to all my clients as it makes it easier to connect to your loved one's energy if you can visualise them effectively.

- Hold a piece of their jewellery, as often it has the vibration of the person it once belonged to and it is easy to get psychic impressions. This technique is called psychometrics and is often used by psychics and mediums.

- When you are ready after a loved one's passing, visit a good, reliable medium as they can make contact as soon as the spirit leaves the body. Once you have made contact, it is easier to connect with them later.

- Try meditation. Once you learn to meditate, it becomes a lot easier to communicate with loved ones and your own angels, guides and spirit helpers. Try to meditate at the same time every day, as it will give you better results.

- Trust that your efforts and good intentions are not in vain. Your loved ones will always make a great effort to get in contact with you in some way, so always follow your intuition and what is best for you.

- Avoid trying to connect with your loved ones when you are overly emotional or confused as this can make it harder to recognise and respond to the subtle shifts in energy which can indicate a loved one's presence.

- Be aware that loved ones often try to make contact during or just after their own funeral. I can't tell you how many times I have seen spirits appearing at their own funeral, either standing next to the coffin or sitting among the congregation. They also like to talk about who was there, what they were dressed in and what songs or hymns were played as validation that they haven't gone too far away, or as proof of survival.

- Be open to subtle spiritual signs: dreams, butterflies, birds, smells, coins, signposts (e.g. street names), numbers, names, smells, to name a few.

Connecting to Past Lives

My first experience with reincarnation was when I was a child. I used to dream continually of a strange land of ice, snow, incredible mountains and large waterways or fjords. After travelling around Europe as a young woman, I ended up in Norway in Scandinavia. As soon as I arrived, I found I had an understanding of the ways and idiosyncrasies of most Norwegian people and felt quite 'at home'. In the large group of international nurses who worked with me in the hospital, I was the only one who understood the language without any problems.

I have always had a photographic memory, but I knew deep down I was certainly no genius and that this knowledge of Norway and the Norwegian culture did not come from any reading or clever understanding of languages, but from a deep and profound knowledge. When I returned to Australia a few years later, I went to a lecture on past life regression therapy and learnt about how we carry memories deep within from past lives. The lecturer told us that her husband had a session with her and he discovered that he had been on the Titanic. Strangely, he had been afraid of the sea and had feared drowning all of his life.

Past Life Regression

The process of connecting to our past lives is referred to as past life regression and is usually achieved through hypnosis with a qualified past life regression therapist.

Although noone is really sure why some people have such strong and demonstrable connections to places, people or cultures of the past, the theory is that, after our physical death, our soul lives on and moves into a new lifetime.

It is an extraordinary experience to recall a past life as it teaches us things about ourselves and can clear phobias and blocks which we have developed through our previous lives or deaths.

Past life regression can also help clear physical issues like bronchial problems, infertility and rashes, to name a few, particularly when used in conjunction with conventional medicine.

In past life regression, the subject answers a series of questions while hypnotised to help reveal their past life identities and associated events. Often, unresolved issues from other past lives, such as phobias, illnesses or unresolved issues in relationships, may be the cause of the subject's present day problems.

When I had my first past life regression, I was taken back to a past life in Norway, where I found I was a huge male Viking called Tron. I was horrified to feel thick hair all over my body, something that I really dislike to this day. In our session I began speaking fluent Norwegian and the therapist asked me to speak in English as she had no idea what I was talking about. In other sessions, I have discovered past lives as a Native American as well as past lives in England and Europe. I use regression regularly in my busy practice and have had the honour to witness many other people's past lives unfurl in front of us. I have learnt a lot about mankind, the spiritual contracts we choose and the soul using this modality.

Recipe for Releasing Past Life Memories
The essences of a number of flower remedies will help you access your past life memories. Below is a recipe I have used several times for a number of clients in my practice, all to great results.

You will need:
> *Empty 25 ml bottle with dropper*
> *Bach flower essences: Honeysuckle, Mimulus, Walnut, Angel Sword, Clematis, Southern Cross*
> *Apple cider*
> *Purified water.*

1. Mix two drops of each of the essences into the empty dropper bottle.
2. Add 5 ml of apple cider and purified water and shake slightly.

3. Allow to settle and store in a cool, dry area out of direct sunlight.
4. Take 2 drops twice a day, morning and night.

This will awaken memories and gifts from other lifetimes and release any unwarranted fears.

Connecting to and Attracting Fairy and Elemental Energy

When was the last time you watched a sunset, sat under a full moon, let the wind blow in your hair and felt the warm touch of the sun caressing your body and skin. Whenever you are feeling rundown, depressed, tired, ungrounded or plain out of sorts, take a long walk in nature and let the nature spirits do their work. By connecting to this powerful energy, you will not only feel rested, but also your aura will be cleansed of any impurities, bringing you back into balance.

Creating a Sacred Space in Nature

Nature is an ideal place to connect to the divine source. Whether it be bush, beach or just a beautiful garden, full of nature's delights, you can more easily connect with the wonderful nature spirits that can bring a sense of joy and light to your life.

The following exercise will help you bring these wonderful entities into your energy field and imbue your aura with their positive light.

1. Find a comfortable place in nature, protected and safe from others. Feel yourself connect to Mother Nature and surround yourself with healing light and loving energy.
2. After a few minutes, you will feel your energy opening and your awareness heighten, raising your vibration.
3. Take your time to breathe in the natural energy and fresh air. Feel it filling your lungs and re-energising your aura.
4. Visualise all your chakras opening up to this wonderful natural energy.

    When you feel totally refreshed, take the time to close down all your chakras, or tiny lights in your energy centres, and thank the Great Spirit for the wisdom and healing. You will feel lighter, and any stresses in the body will be lifted.

Healing with Your Own Fairy Garden

Having a fairy garden is a must for children and the child within us as it is the most perfect way of attracting beautiful energy. Not only is it mystical, but also decorative and healing — the perfect place to visit when feeling down in the dumps. It is also the ideal place to relocate plants to when they aren't flourishing elsewhere as the energy from the nature spirits is energising and healing for all natural things.

If you live in a flat or smaller space without a garden, you can create a fairy garden pot, which is just as effective and brings much needed natural energy into urban spaces.

It can be placed in a small space on a veranda or near a window and you can have all sorts of bits and pieces in your pot, but not too much clutter as this will cause obstacles to the flow of energy.

By creating a space in your garden or pot, you will attract positive energy from the elemental kingdom that will look after your home and bring you harmonious energy.

If you believe and look long enough, you might just see a gnome tending your vegetables, or a light fairy shaking a lonely leaf on a tree when there is no wind. Even if you don't see these lovely little creatures, their free light-hearted energy will add laughter and joy to your whole home.

Exercise: Setting up your fairy garden

First off, you need the right spot for your fairy garden. Choose somewhere private, preferably that is shady and quiet.

If there are particular elemental energies you hope to attract, try placing your garden near natural features to attract those specific creatures. Both my fairy gardens are next to trees. I have one near a fishpond and in the other a lovely bird bath to attract healing emotional water energy.

I also have little colourful flowers and small hardy shrubs and ferns that are easy to maintain to create a great spot for the hard-working gnome energy. In the surrounding trees, I have placed wind chimes, as these are an invitation to the sylph or air spirits and attract lots of butterflies and various types of birds.

You may also like to include little lights, which look very charming, especially at night, and can attract the fiery, passionate energy of the salamander.

Around your garden place a few statues of fairies, unicorns, gnomes, devas and elves. You might also like to include a tiny house, which will energetically send out a lovely welcome to all the fairies to visit the garden. Visitors, particularly children, love to visit my fairy garden, and they too are welcome as long as they are quiet and respectful. It is, after all, an energetic portal to another realm and needs to be respected. Don't be surprised, though, if your pets also choose to spend a lot of time there, as the natural energies calm and soothe all creatures.

Attracting Angels

Elemental and spirit guide energy is wonderful to have around you to protect and heal your space. But if you want really powerful energy, then calling on angelic realms for the love and protection of angels will banish any sense of energetic blockage or darkness that may be hanging about.

Angels want to assist us, but it is useful to know them and how to attract the specific angel energy that will be most beneficial for you.

Connecting with the Archangels

There are many types of angels but the four Archangels come from the highest order and are closest to God. We are all blessed to know and understand that they are of service to mankind and will help you anytime you ask. I always have an angel altar in my home and place of work for protection, friendship and assistance.

Archangel Michael

Michael, whom I affectionately call the 'bouncer boy' of the archangels, is a strong warrior archetype with powerful and sometimes overwhelming masculine energy. When you call on his assistance, you will feel incredibly safe, as if he is wrapping his mighty huge wings around you with great but gentle force.

His gift is protection against psychic attack and the ability to let go of any negative emotions and move forward when you are feeling stuck in your life or having ongoing problems. I have called on him when I have had an emergency in my life and when I have been under attack from nasty cyber bullying.

In my spirit rescue work I am always calling on him for assistance and without fail I always get results. When you visualise him, he appears with a silver sword and shield, cutting through any negative matter or dark energy that may be sent your way. No matter what the challenge or what you are going through, all you have to do is ask for his help as he is always ready to protect and serve humanity in any way.

Archangel Raphael

This is the angel of healing and protection. His name means *God heals*. This angel is also known as the patron of healers and those in need of healing. When we call in this incredible energy, any problems we may have with health, work or money will generally clear.

Invoking this angel also brings peace to others. Light workers, healers and counsellors all over the world call on him in their work. It is believed that this mighty Archangel is able to fearlessly move into whatever area is needed in healing, bringing a host of angels with him to accomplish this. When I have channelled this angel, I have felt a very strong green energy in the room.

Archangel Uriel

This angel's name means *Light of God* and he brings divine light and healing of painful burdens from the past into our lives. Allow the light of wisdom of this angel to shine on your subconscious mind. I call this angel the Archangel of forgiveness as his energy helps release anger, resentment and past memories, which can cause mental pain and illness.

This is a good energy to use when you want to surrender as you are invoking pure love that will soon fill your soul with balance and peace. This energy helps you to anchor spiritual understanding as it brings harmony to chaotic situations and creates an easier path to the healing process. To me this is a gentle, subtle and soft energy with an incredible amount of pure, all consuming sheer light which feels quite blinding.

Archangel Gabriel

Archangel Gabriel is the *bringer of good news and hope*. I call this energy my special magic; it helps me manifest whatever I may need in the physical world. I have worked with this angelic energy many times throughout the years and it is different every time. When you call on this energy, you will receive great wisdom and love, which is required to evolve to a higher good when working in the service of mankind.

Connecting to Angels in Our Daily Lives

Once you connect to the angels, you will be amazed by how many ways they can help you. As light workers, most of us forget to look after ourselves and angels are happy to protect and nourish us as we help others connect to light and love.

These are some of the ways angelic energy can manifest in our lives:

1. Angels create a feeling of fun and joy. They remind us not to take life so seriously, to learn to have fun and laugh more as creativity comes from humour, and that not letting go of the small stuff only keeps us blocked and unhappy.
2. They create a sense of meaning in our lives — a deep knowledge that life as we know it is precious and meant to be lived to the fullest.
3. Angels remind us that for a successful life we need to bring more joy and play into our lives so our spiritual contracts on earth are easier. They also remind us that life is beautiful like the colours of nature.
4. Angels ask us only to trust and love ourselves unconditionally.
5. They only assist us when asked; they never intervene, as they need our permission. The good thing is we can call on them as often as we wish.

As life is a constant journey of highs and lows and sometimes very hard lessons, I have learnt that angels can help us in many ways we never dreamt of. If, in any part of your life you need help, call on them.

Exercise: Asking angels for assistance

You will need:

A quiet private room or space

A rose quartz crystal

A small hand mirror or dressing table mirror.

1. Stand in front of a mirror holding the rose quartz crystal in your hands.
2. Stare deeply into your eyes and say very slowly with meaning, love and an open heart, a bit of trust, and a whole lot of knowing of what you really want until any doubts or fears are released with a suitable affirmation, and you will attract the right vibration/person into your life.
3. Clearly recite the affirmation based on what you wish to manifest.

On the following pages are the perfect affirmations for specific areas and vibrations of angelic energy.

Angels of New Beginnings

Sometimes we feel as if we are stuck and not learning the lessons or spiritual contracts we asked for in heaven.

Call the Angel of Clarity and Compassion and ask:

Help me move forward and have a breakthrough with work and life. Or show me a path so my heart can sing with success.

Angels of Work Opportunities

In these days of insecure work and rising competition, this affirmation can be very handy. I don't know how many times I have asked this particular angel for help only to have a great opportunity manifest very soon afterwards.

Say out loud:

Angel of Promotion, please assist me to get the job I need. I have worked so hard for a break, as I love the work I do, and am ready to learn new things.

Or:

Angel of New Job Opportunity, please come and assist me now that I am ready for new work.

Angels of Protection

I always use this angelic energy, along with white light energy, whenever I need protection or help. You can also use it for keeping your loved ones safe and protecting your car and home.

Say out loud:

Angels of Protection, please help me find the strength I have within me to do what I need to do, and keep me safe as I fulfil my spiritual contract.

Angels of Finance

Angels of Finance, please help me find a way to help pay off my bills. I wish to get ahead financially and save some money for a rainy day.

Angels of Family

Angels of Happy Families, please help with the problems we are having so we may love, learn to communicate, support and live in harmony with each other.

Angels of Health

Angels of Health, please assist, guide and help me live a better life.

Angels of Love Relationships

Angels of Love Relationships, please help me find my soulmate, I am now ready to move forward and embrace love in its highest form.

Angels of Peace and Harmony

Angels of Peace and Harmony, please bring more love and harmony to the planet and everyone on it. May we all live together in peace and love.

Once you have completed your affirmation, thank the angels for their help.

Exercise: Write a letter to your angels

Angels can help you in so many ways, if you communicate what you want. An effective way to manifest angel energy is to write an angelic letter detailing what you want to create and embrace in your life. This will also help you focus and show gratitude for the wonderful things you already enjoy.

You will need:

> *A quiet writing space*
> *Good quality paper or journal*
> *Pen.*

1. To start, imagine your writing space filled with white light to protect you as you connect with the angelic realm.

2. Take up your pen and paper and start to write from your heart what you would like to tell your angel guardians. When writing to your angels, be as detailed and specific as possible and make sure to note the time, date and year of writing so you can document how long it takes to receive an answer.

3. Once you have finished the letter, energise the paper with an additional burst of white light energy and visualise that energy taking your words up to your angel guides. Close the book or fold the paper and store in a specific drawer or box. Remember to thank your angels as you secure your letter.

As you practise more, you will learn to work with angels and understand that they can help you in many ways you never dreamed of. When you start to incorporate angels into your life, you will never look back and will wonder how you survived without them. Just remember to thank them when they reply with a sign or symbol of love and blessing.

Working with Healing Angels

As light workers, we must always ask the person's higher self for permission before we do any type of energy work or healing. It is not permissible by the universal laws to do so without permission. Before you proceed with whatever type of healing energy you wish to use, ask for concentrated thought towards the Lord Christ, as this is the most powerful healing in the universe and the angels work with this energy.

As a spiritualist for many years, before I practise any healing, psychic, energy or spiritual work, I always say a little prayer before I invoke the energies. Others may have their own prayers to the goddess.

I am a clear and perfect channel of light
Let love and light be my guide, thank you.

Once the healing power has been invoked, always with the fullest faith, the outcome should be left to the karma and evolutionary needs of the individual. Always surrender to the divine will, or the will of God, not personal will, as the energy will be tenfold stronger.

One should remember when working with great forces that, in no circumstances, should anyone use their willpower and occult knowledge to obtain by force any personal or material benefits for oneself or for others as this energy represents grey or black magic. I have found over the years that people who work with this type of energy never prosper, tending to have little love in their lives, illness, money issues or continual blocked issues to do with energy.

Exercise: Connecting to angelic healing

You will need:

A quiet space to meditate.

1. Open up your energies by doing a chakra meditation.
2. Once you have opened up your energies and surrendered to the higher powers, surround yourself and your patient with a white light.
3. Close your eyes and use the palms of your hands to direct streams of purified energy into and through the aura of the sufferer to disperse congestion in the etheric and emotional bodies to drive out harmful substances. This will restore the harmonious and rhythmic flow of the client's life forces, which are out of alignment due to illness. This may take time if the client has been sick for a long period.
4. Once you have done this, invoke the higher energies by calling in your mind's eye the healing angels and the Christ energy and leave the healing to the invisible force of the angels and the higher powers that be.
5. Once you feel the energy has diminished, close yourself down and give thanks, light and blessings.

Creating an Angel Altar

Throughout my life I have created many sacred altars to help with manifestation, abundance, protection and prayer. I now have one in my place of work, my meditation room and my bedroom. My intention has always been to create portholes of divine light in these areas to welcome in my guides and my angel helpers.

I have also created abundance by using the energy of Ganesh and the three prosperity goddesses, Lakshmi, Fortuna and Abundantia. Love, protection and light have now been generated in my busy office, my beautiful meditation room and my bedroom to help me with my dreams.

Exercise: Build your own altar to sit by at least
once a day

To build your own altar to sit by at least once a day,

You will need:
> Small table or bench
> Clean white cloth
> Flowers, plants
> Objects sacred to you, such as photographs, shells, statues of angels
> A white candle.

1. Find a small table or bench and cover it with the clean white cloth.

2. Ask your angels to join you as you create this special, beautiful work of art.

3. Next decorate it with fresh flowers and plants, pictures, statues of angels, animals and fairies, crystals, rocks, shells, feathers, icons, incense burner, candles — whatever suits your fancy.

4. I always use incense and essential oils for a special aroma. Harps and flute music, or bells, attract loving angels into your sacred space, but any calming, relaxing music will do.

5. When your altar is finished, light the white candle on the altar as this will invoke healing heavenly energy.

You can ask to attract angelic energy in general or choose to work with the Archangels Michael, Uriel, Rafael and Gabriel for stronger energy, as these beings are very powerful.

If ever my altar needs clearing, I give it a good sage and gently filter the smoke through with a feather.

Exercise: Angel meditation

This meditation exercise is helpful when you want to connect to angelic energy for healing, protection or space clearing.

You will need:

A quiet space where you won't be disturbed

Optional: A blanket or pillow for comfort.

1. Find yourself a quiet space where you will not be disturbed. Sit up nice and straight and breath deeply three times to centre yourself.

2. Feel yourself relaxing as you slowly breathe in and out, relaxing with each breath you take.

3. As you visualise your chakras, imagine them opening, starting from the root chakra at the base of the spine (a red colour).

4. Now work your way up to your sacral chakra, which is orange, your solar plexus chakra, which is yellow, your heart, which is green, your throat chakra, which is blue, your third eye, which is indigo, and finally your crown chakra, which is violet.

5. Now imagine, you have come to a most beautiful garden, a place of peace, tranquility and unconditional love, deep within your soul.

6. Once you have done this, sit down gently on soft green grass as you continue to breathe in a relaxed manner. Feel yourself fill with light and love, and know that you are completely centred.

7. Focusing your intention, begin to call in the Archangels. Call upon the Archangel Michael, the 'big bouncer' of the angels. Ask him to present himself to you. As you do so, let go of any fear and distrust in your higher self. Let go of any negative emotions that may block your spiritual sight. Feel his loving energy as he stands next to you.

8. Call on the Archangel Gabriel so that you receive the wisdom and love required to evolve to a higher good. Feel his loving energy as he stands next to you.

9. Call on Archangel Raphael. Feel his loving energy as he stands next to you, for all that is hidden is now known as your intuition. You now have clarity of vision.

10. Call on Archangel Uriel. Allow his light and wisdom to shine down on you. Feel his love as he stands next to you.

11. Now it is time to call upon your guardian angel. Is it male or female or androgynous? What does your angel feel like? Is there a message or gift for you? Feel your loving angel's energy.

12. Ask now for a healing, then ask that any negative energy or unwanted cords be cut out of your aura and body and anything else that you no longer need in your life.

13. Now it is time to say goodbye until the next time you want to call upon your angels for love and support. Thank the Archangels for being present and remember to close down your chakras, which are like little lights, and wrap white light around you.

Final Thoughts

Working with energy and energetic beings is a great gift and will bring you many blessings and opportunities. If you do it right. It is my hope that this book has helped you on the path of connecting to the divine around you and feeling safe and secure in your space.

RECOMMENDED READING

Edward Bach

The Twelve Healers

Alicen & Neil Geddes-Ward

Faeriecraft: Treading the Path of Faerie Magic

Kerrie Erwin

Magical Tales of the Forest

Memoirs of a Suburban Medium

Sacred Signs

Sacred Soul

Sacred Space

Spirits Whispering in My Ear

Tarot for Light Workers

Dr Michael Newton

Destiny of the Souls

Memories of the Afterlife

Elizabeth Clare Prophet

How to Work with Angels

Is Mother Nature Mad? How to Work with Nature Spirits to Mitigate Natural Disasters.

Mary Magdalene and the Divine Feminine

Kerrie Erwin's books are available on her website, at selected bookstores and as eBooks on Kindle and Amazon.

SPIRITUAL MEDIUM, CLAIRVOYANT AND
INTERNATIONAL AUTHOR
KERRIE ERWIN

www.pureview.com.au

Sydney-based medium Kerrie Erwin has lived between two worlds since childhood and is able to *see* and *hear* spirit people talking. Realising her true calling when she was very young, she now works professionally as a spiritual medium and clairvoyant, focusing on spirit rescue, hauntings and connecting people to loved ones who have passed over into the spirit world. She also teaches metaphysics, reads tarot cards and works with Feng Shui, and is trained in spiritual hypnotherapies and past-life regression. She works all over Australia via phone, Skype and the media.

Closely aligned with Kerrie's healing work is her vibrant creative nature. Coming from a media background, she has hosted her own show on Cable TV, *Let»s Have a Chat with Kerrie*, has had guest appearances on Channel 7 and *All About You*, and has worked on and off for Psychic TV. She also regularly works in club shows and appears on radio around the country.

Kerrie has also written several books, writes a column for the *Sydney Observer* and contributes to other publications.

Her aim as a spiritual medium is to help as many people as possible to teach others that love is eternal and to inspire them to believe in themselves.